IT ALMOST SEEMS SIMPLE

IT ALMOST SEEMS SIMPLE

Who Knew Creating a National Brand Could Be This Much Fun?

Susan Spann

Cover photo: Charlie McCullers
Interior photos courtesy: Walt Lincer, Syl Harris, Susan Spann

ISBN-13: 9781540642165
ISBN-10: 154064216X
Library of Congress Control Number: 2017901477
CreateSpace Independent Publishing Platform
North Charleston, South Carolina

With thanks to Syl Harris and Walt Lincer for providing unlimited access to years of stories, verifications, and entertaining recollections.

Contents

This is a work of nonfiction. I was a firsthand observer of many of the events related here. Syl Harris and Walt Lincer provided insights and memories and did fact checking throughout. This book uses remembered conversations—which are obviously not meant to be taken as verbatim—telephone conversations, and also pieces of early interviews and videos conducted or made when the Florida's Natural brand was young. Where appropriate, sources are cited.

Many corroborating pieces came from Internet research that included competitive and industry history. Other information came from industry data, also widely available on the Internet.

Thanks to the generous contributions from Syl and Walt, I was able to tell a story with sometimes differing viewpoints yet mostly complementary details, differences that add depth and dimension to the story.

Introduction

While working at Tucker Wayne Advertising in the 1980s, I had the privilege of working on the Citrus World account and being part of the team that launched the Florida's Natural brand. Until I got assigned to that piece of business, I had seen the typical side of account service. Most of the work involved keeping the people in the creative department happy so that they would keep the clients happy. Account-service people walked the line between these two entities. My fortune and my view of the job changed when I was assigned to work for Syl Harris. Since he hadn't come into the agency business in a traditional way (i.e., through a marketing or advertising degree), Syl brought a different kind of analysis and attitude to solving day-to-day account problems. It helped that he was not a schemer and had no ulterior motives other than delivering the best work he could. He was rational, calm, and could always figure out alternate ways to get something done. I'll admit that sometimes when I went to him in frustration, trying to figure out how to do the impossible, he calmed me by breaking the task down into little pieces so we could move forward. He also taught me the art of diplomacy. More than once, I brought Syl a letter that I was about to send to a client or to a vendor who had not delivered (these were the days of typing letters that did not fall victim to a hasty Send button—correspondence could be reread and rethought), and he backed me off on the language and showed me how to calm down my overwrought, emotional tone.

And Syl gave me real-world exposure and opportunities as well. I worked for another supervisor before him who never allowed me to travel to meet a client. Within one week of being assigned to the Citrus World account, I was booked on a plane to Florida, first class no less (it was the 1980s!), so Syl could introduce me to Walt Lincer and his team. It was the start of a long-term relationship.

I had been warned about Walt. I had been told that he was quick to make a judgment; that he hadn't liked the previous account executive; that I should ignore some of the quick, sometimes hurtful remarks he would make about our strategy and about our work; and that everything would be fine. I was nervous and excited to travel to Citrus World. It was such a milestone that I even remember what I wore to the meeting and what I ate for breakfast on the plane on the short trip from Atlanta to Orlando. After all, it was my first trip in first class.

Syl and I landed in Orlando and headed down to Lake Wales. Traveling with Syl was always a bit like traveling with Dad. He drove, he paid, he explained, he made sure things went smoothly. And he set a great example. At that first meeting, I sat quietly at the conference-room table and watched as Syl presented artwork, layouts, and media plans. I watched how he handled Walt's objections, when he disagreed, and when he rolled over. I saw Walt flip immediately to the back page of a presentation to see how much the work would cost; cutting Syl off before he could open his mouth. I saw the way Syl managed to convince Walt to try what was being proposed without ever seeming argumentative. In fact, Syl always seemed agreeable. And he always was. To say I learned a lot from Syl barely covers it.

Naturally, Walt has read through this book. I've heard him rant, "Great. Syl looks like Mother Theresa while I'm going around burning down orphanages!" But Walt's style had a charm of its own and was so very instructive. Watching Walt work, watching him move through the office making quick decisions, and listening to him following his gut even when the research numbers didn't quite agree was instruction of another sort. And it kind of spoiled me for working with other clients. If something didn't make sense to Walt or for the company, even if it made sense to the rest of the world, he would question it and come up with an alternative plan. Once the team got the Florida's Natural brand moving, Walt was always mindful of the fact that it was like Tropicana and Minute Maid in substance only. The company, the process, the advertising, and the budget were unique to Florida's Natural. We had to always be mindful of that and couldn't model ourselves after anyone else, mostly because the company simply couldn't afford it.

Thinking back over the work I've done for Citrus World over the past thirty years, including the projects I worked on once I switched from full-time account service to be a special-projects freelancer, I realized that the Florida's Natural story is a unique one. It's not the story of a massive new high-tech business where billions of dollars of wealth are created. It's not the story of an invention that somehow changed our planet. It's simply the story of a dedicated group of people taking on the two biggest beverage companies in the world and somehow succeeding. It's *Hoosiers*; it's the 1980 US hockey team against the Russians. It's David facing down two Goliaths.

Walt retired in December of 2012. By then, the Florida's Natural brand had achieved record volume, distribution, and market share combined with the highest rates of grower return and consumer loyalty in the history of Citrus World. Plus, the brand had grown into a $600-million-plus business.

When Syl retired in March of 2013, I approached him and asked him if he'd like to help me convince Walt to share the story. Syl agreed.

"Why would I want to do that?" Walt reacted. Syl and I pushed; Walt caved, which was not the usual result of our conversations. And when we all started talking, out poured the events, strategies, personalities, struggles, and victories that affirmed our thinking that there was value in telling this tale.

At the heart of this history is a story of a brand, the team who brought it to life, and the man who engineered it all. Odds did not favor the success or even the longevity of the Florida's Natural brand. But loyal customers have kept it on the shelves for almost thirty years. The big dogs have had to make way for the underdog.

And who doesn't like a story about an underdog?

1

Walt Comes to Citrus World

Citrus World had a problem. It needed a juice brand of its own. For more than fifty years, this growers' cooperative had been selling citrus juice. It had many products, and its flagship brand, Donald Duck Orange Juice, was well known in many parts of the country. But Donald Duck was licensed from the Walt Disney Company. Two established regional brands, Bluebird and Texsun, had been acquired and were doing well in the international and domestic canned juice segments. But they weren't enough. What the company needed was to create its own brand of refrigerated juice that could be competitive in the market. Company executives were just not quite sure how to go about doing this. And they weren't quite sure what that brand should be. They needed some experience and some fresh thinking on the subject.

When Walt Lincer joined the company, they at least got fresh thinking.

WALT LINCER, FORMER VP OF SALES AND MARKETING FOR CITRUS WORLD

This story really has lots of layers, and I guess the first one is how I got to Citrus World.

I grew up in Phoenix and had the good fortune to attend an all-boys Jesuit prep school. My parents were not college graduates, but they made sure all their kids got the best education available. My mom actually took in ironing to help pay my tuition at Brophy Prep, realizing the value of a Jesuit education. The Jesuits teach you how to think.

After high school, I followed a winding path, eventually ending up at the University of Denver, where I studied marketing. But Denver was my second try at college. I had attended Arizona State University for a short time with the idea of becoming a doctor. My only interest in medicine was that doctors made a lot of money. As a kid from a typical working-class family, I was determined to succeed at something that paid well. Unfortunately for me, premed involved classes like organic chemistry, where you actually had to know something.

I had followed my sister to Arizona State University. She was a brilliant student, and my plan was to take all the same classes she took from the same professors. I would use her notes and old tests. One of those classes was entomology. Fifty percent of the final grade was determined by classifying one hundred insects down to genus and species. I spent the night before the big project was due rearranging the bugs in my sister's bug box with new labels. She got an A; I got a B. I guess I could hardly complain.

In 1967, organic chemistry got me an invitation to join the US Army. I was sure I was perfect for the Quartermaster Corps. The army, however, felt my talents were better suited to being an infantryman. In reality, I was too immature for college. The army makes you grow up fast. Two years in the infantry and then as a drill sergeant helped me see that my military future was not bright, so I went back to college. This time, I studied marketing. I quickly realized marketing was 80 percent common sense and 20 percent bullshit. It was my calling—I had found something I liked and was good at—especially the BS.

Drill Sergeant Walter Lincer

During one summer vacation, I worked for *Readers' Digest*. The magazine was doing an annual Fourth of July promotion and had hired students to sell displays of food products that were advertised in the July issue. Each of us was assigned a number of grocery stores and had to convince the store managers that they really needed to display the products featured in the *Reader's Digest* insert.

I had twenty stores that summer, and I managed to sell displays to eighteen of them. It bugged me that I couldn't get the other two. But when the season ended and I got the award for selling the most, I was stunned to learn that the next highest salesperson only managed to sell three or four displays. At that point, I realized that I had to go into marketing and sales. It was easy—all you had to do was work hard!

It was tough graduating from college in 1972. The recession meant that few companies were hiring and that it might not be so easy to get the perfect job. But getting to that point had been a long haul for me, and I was ready to start working. Somehow, I got interviews at Proctor and Gamble (P&G) and Lever Brothers. I guess I wasn't smart or pedigreed enough for P&G, but Lever Brothers hired me, and I stayed there for seven years.

I came out of college with high expectations that I would be making major decisions on how brands were marketed. Imagine my surprise when I was handed a feather duster and a box cutter. I had four promotions during my time working there, and I moved four times, eventually ending up as an operations analyst at the corporate office on Park Avenue making $24,000 a year. While I was visiting markets, writing evaluations, and making systems recommendations, I noticed that the most junior brand-marketing guy was making twice as much as me. This confirmed my idea that marketing and brand management was where I needed to be. But for those jobs, Lever only hired graduates from top-tier schools who were long on credentials and short on street sense.

Lever separated its brand-management and sales departments. They were two separate management chains. The sales people lived in their markets and were pragmatic and flexible. They had to compete with P&G, which had all the number-one-selling brands. The marketing people were Ivy League types who competed with each other to make the snarkiest comments about anyone they perceived to be beneath them, which in their minds was the whole sales force. Marketing people seldom visited customers or markets. If they did, it was usually to dine at the finest local restaurant. They rarely listened to sales people. I always felt one of the reasons Lever Brothers couldn't compete in the United States against P&G was because of the New York City types who stayed hunkered down at their Park Avenue headquarters. I knew that if I were ever in charge, brand management and sales would report to the same person.

I started as a retail manager, which involved calling on stores to check on the placement and distribution of our products. It was a very low-level job but a very valuable learning experience. Retail is where the purchase decision is made. If you are wrong at retail, you are dead. My first management job was running a dysfunctional retail unit in Arizona. This group of stores had finished last out of twenty-five western-region units in sales of our products for four consecutive years. During my three years as manager, it finished no worse than second out of twenty-five units. My secret—I worked sixty hours a week and didn't follow the rules exactly as they were written. Or I should say, I liberally interpreted the rules.

I had the good fortune to have Dan Womack as my first boss. Dan was a Texan who played football at the University of Georgia. He had presence. He was six feet two in every direction, with no neck and a head the size of a basketball. On one of Dan's corporate moves, his house was burglarized. Nearly everything he owned was stolen, including his wardrobe. The cops found his size-fifty-eight clothing in a Goodwill bin. After one look at the size, the thieves realized those things were useless to them. Dan was a sales manager who knew and used every trick. He viewed selling soap like playing a football game; he wanted to win. The company had no idea that he manipulated the various brands' promotional funds, but it wasn't unusual for him to use Drive detergent money to sell Aim toothpaste. He only cared about making the number.

Making the number refers to reaching or surpassing the sales quota. It was the key to being promoted in Dan's eyes. I always made my number.

I marveled at Dan's creativity. For example, he decided to launch a Lever fabric softener in Los Angeles. The brand was Final Touch. It was a no-name product and a distant, distant second to P&G's Downy. Dan found out that Lever had some obsolete eight-ounce bottles of Final Touch—a few thousand cases. He had the sales force pitch three sizes of Final Touch to every account in Los Angeles. The key selling point he made was that one million samples would be dropped at residences on a given Saturday, which was nowhere near true. I think it was more like two thousand. He had his son's Boy Scout troop hang the sample bottles on the doors of the buyers' residences and their neighbors' one Saturday. Needless to say—every account authorized Final Touch.

One problem was that Lever only made two sizes. The third size we presented didn't exist. Dan's idea was if we offered three, they would turn down one size. Naturally, some accounts wanted the size we didn't have. Dan actually had the guts to request that the company make the size that didn't exist, but in the end, we got every account to take two sizes—the sizes we already had.

Selling soap was a great learning experience. Competing against P&G and Colgate was not unlike competing with Coke and Pepsi. I learned a lot about what to do and what not to do. The arrogance of P&G was our key benefit to the trade. Because P&G had all the number-one brands, like Tide detergent and Crest toothpaste, their sales people forced retailers to buy and promote their second-tier brands to get allocations of the number-one brands. The trade used us as a counterweight to P&G.

For about a year, I commuted to New York City from Phoenix every week. Eventually, the company realized I hadn't moved to New York though they wanted me to. When I resisted, they offered me a position in Chicago. I abruptly resigned.

Instead, I took a job as director of sales and marketing for a little juice company in Fullerton, California, called Polar Chill; it was owned by a Florida processor called Southern Gold. I was a little skeptical—after all, I was leaving a major corporation. "Is this company solid?" I asked the president, who hired me. This was in the days before the Internet. Knowledge of a small company was much harder to come by.

"Rock solid" was the reply, which turned out to mean the company was insolvent.

Six weeks later, Polar Chill was sold to Citrus World and renamed World Citrus West.

A few weeks after that, I met Joe Marshburn, Citrus World CEO, and Bob Turner, VP of marketing. Joe would later tell me that my hire was a contingency in the presale terms between Southern Gold and Citrus World. I remember Bob Turner saying, "We will keep you, but don't expect a pay raise." As a newly married man, I needed a solid job, so I immediately began looking for a new opportunity. I was offered a position with a large multinational company. But before accepting it, I started digging into Citrus World's operations. I soon realized that they were so backward and disorganized that working for them was a perfect opportunity.

• • •

Citrus World had no real sales or marketing plans. In a world where marketing was king, they were a production company.

WALT

The first sales guy I met was actually introduced to me as Citrus World's number-one salesperson and was known by his nickname, Rotten, which was an acronym he used on a business card. He actually had two business cards, one listing his title correctly as regional manager. The other, which he used to impress people, said general manager. Rotten was out of central casting. He was a music-man type of traveling sales manager—always ready with an off-color joke or story, even when inappropriate. He loved golf and was terrible at it. He hit his drives 135 yards. But he dressed the part. He bragged that he had over one hundred coordinated golf outfits. One time, he drove a hundred miles to buy turquoise golf shoes. Rotten had developed the Arizona market for Donald Duck, where Donald Duck frozen concentrate became the number-one brand. Rotten gave this market special attention. Oh yeah—his girlfriend lived there.

A week after meeting Rotten, I met the national sales manager, who had been hired away from his job as a buyer at A&P. He was supposed to bring A&P's private-label frozen business to Citrus World. He didn't. He was not a very sharp guy. At our first meeting we went to dinner. We had drinks, or should I say, he drank. A lot. I guess he didn't notice that I don't drink. Before long, he was drunk, and I got him talking. He told me all about the payoffs he took as a buyer. For example, a pickle company had built his pool. He told me he had lots of ideas for the sales force, but he actually had none. If this guy was the national sales manager, then opportunity was knocking!

The top salesman and the sales manager didn't know anything about marketing or how to organize a sales force. The company was bumbling along, making deals, and hiring friends and relatives who promised to bring in business. There were no goals. There was no plan, no focus. For example, when I asked what the policies were for expense accounts, I was told, "We won't buy your women, but we will buy your women dinner." The personal conduct policy was "Don't get your name in the paper."

After three months at World Citrus West, Joe Marshburn and Bob Turner asked me to come to Florida to start a brand and to build a branded sales division. Of course, I agreed because they offered me more money. Plus, the job was in Florida. That was a bonus—no state income tax and low-cost housing! I thought naively, "How hard can it be to start a new brand?" I soon found out.

I clearly remember telling my wife about the new opportunity in Central Florida. She was a trooper but not really thrilled about moving to a small Florida town from Southern California. When we got there, we both were stunned by the difference in culture. After her first trip to the local Publix Supermarket, she came home to relate her experience. The clerk actually engaged her in conversation, asking for and sharing all kinds of personal details. Darleene said, "Walt, we're not in Kansas anymore." That year, we went to the annual citrus festival, a sort of county fair. When we saw some of the local folks, we were shocked. They didn't dress, act, or sound anything like our neighbors across the country. But after living in

Polk County for a year, we found the people to be wonderful, and it turned out to be a great place to raise our kids.

Walt with family

Around this time, the sales manager suddenly resigned. He said he could see the writing on the wall and that I would be his boss. Suddenly, I was in charge of sales for the whole company.

In those days, about 90 percent of the company's business was in private label products and 10 percent was in Donald Duck. I soon learned that after discounts to the buyers were subtracted, the brand was sold cheaper than private label products.

Donald Duck had been part of the Citrus World roster since the late 1940s. The company licensed the image and the name from the Walt Disney Company and paid a royalty. For years, Donald's face was on our cans, bottles, and cartons. Donald

Duck juice was a from-concentrate brand, and for years, it was the major branded product the company carried. But a brand that was licensed from the Walt Disney Company would only take the company so far. Donald Duck sold at a lower price than other branded products. Between the discounts we handed out to retailers and the fees we paid to Disney for licensing, it was a drag on the company. We were practically losing money with every case sold. The amazing thing was that the cost systems were so antiquated that management didn't know it.

Citrus World was started in 1933 by a group of fresh-fruit packinghouses that needed an outlet for fruit that could not be sold as fresh. Growers who supplied Citrus World with fruit formed a cooperative and banded together to sell what they grew. The fruit went to the co-op, which produced juice. The co-op was obligated to take all the fruit the members delivered. Most of it was processed into canned juice and later, frozen concentrate. If they had too much product, they would cut the price. If they had too little, they just stopped selling.

The sales force worked half a year to sell the crop. Once they sold to all their private-label customers, they shut down selling for the rest of the year and managed the bookings. As far as I could tell, that meant they took long lunches and played lots of golf.

I came from a company with a lot of structure to one with none.

• • •

Imagining the first days of a Walt-Lincer-led sales department brings a combination of smiles and sympathy for the poor souls who suddenly found themselves—and their jobs—redefined. Walt is a blend of intelligence, humor, shrewd judgment, and impatience. He appreciates quick thinking and sound strategies. But there is little tolerance for poor execution. His new position at Citrus World gave him carte blanche to follow a field plan that he himself created.

WALT

I spent my early days at Citrus World trying to come up with a plan for the sales group. The first thing I did was to look through an old sales manual from my time at Lever Brothers. In the first few years, I basically lifted many of Lever's organizational lessons and applied them to Citrus World.

Lever had quotas. I thought, "Oh, quotas! That's a good idea!" And they had an incentive plan. I thought we should try that too. Each time I introduced something, management thought I was a genius. Remember—they had no plan at all. I developed a weekly report system where they actually had to account for their time. There had been no measurement of activity, no logs, nothing. The salespeople came to work each day, made a few calls, went out to lunch, and every now and then sold some product. They did the minimum.

I developed a policy manual with guidelines for a professional sales force taken directly from the old Lever sales manual. There were things in there like sales and reporting terminology and details of expectations. There were also pages dedicated to fundamental items like how to dress.

I was trying to build a house with just a hammer and a nail. But at least I had a place to start.

2

The Account Guy

A young Syl Harris hard at work

While Walt was finding his way at Citrus World, a young guy in Atlanta was being groomed for account work at an ad agency. But his training did not prepare him for the twists and turns that lay ahead.

In 1986, Syl Harris was thirty-four years old and had already been working in advertising for twelve years. Syl was a big guy, a former football player who was way too nice to ever be successful in that sport. In fact, Syl's overall niceness was the first thing you noticed about him. He had tons of friends and the respect of the entire agency. Syl was fair, patient, and loyal, and everyone wanted to work for him. He was also a player and coach of the company's softball team, and everyone wanted to be a part of it. In spite of the old adage, this nice guy eventually led his team to a first-place finish in the ad league championship.

Syl was also very eager to please, which turned out to be a valuable characteristic when working with Walt.

SYL HARRIS, FORMER EVP AND GROUP ACCOUNT DIRECTOR FOR 22SQUARED

When I first met Walt, he recommended that I read the book *The Art of War* by Sun Tzu. So, I figured the faster I read, it the better off I would be. And I did, in fact, gain a lot of insight into Walt's approach to marketing, strategizing, creating tactics, positioning, maneuvering, and attacking, and in particular, finding opportunities through the weakness of the enemy. We actually used many of these "arts" to guide us over the years.

Citrus World had been using Bob Byars, an older gentleman on the West Coast, as a consultant, and he helped them advertise Donald Duck juice in the markets that were already developed. Bob had a world of experience working on huge consumer brands for top-tier agencies. The ads he created for Citrus World were simple and effective newspaper coupons, sales sheets, and even a couple of television spots. Donald Duck was doing okay. But then the company wanted to expand the brand's distribution. In the summer of 1985, Bob believed he had taken it as far as he could and graciously suggested that they hire a full-service ad agency.

We were invited to pitch. I wasn't in on it, but I heard that aside from our agency, there was an outfit from Tampa in the running for the account. That group had actually become Walt's first choice. They were in Florida and were a good size. Walt liked the account rep and was ready to sign them. He invited Citrus World's CEO, Joe Marshburn, and the VP of marketing, Bob Turner, to attend the final pitch. Walt was sure the meeting would just be a formality since all had been going so well. But then the agency president, whom the Citrus World team had never met, joined the group in the conference room and proceeded to unsell his agency to the Citrus World guys. He knew nothing about their business and was so condescending to them that they were completely turned off. He acted like he was presenting to a bunch of local yokels from Hooterville on *Green Acres*.

In the meantime, my agency's president, Knox Massey, and the senior account executive were waiting outside to make their final presentation. Apparently, Knox came in with no speech and no grand agenda. He was casual, easy, and welcoming. We had already shown our talent, and this sealed the deal. The way Walt tells it, he was shocked that the other agency lost the account. He asked the account rep why he had let his boss come in to the pitch. "What could I do?" he asked. "He's the president of the company!" Well, that president talked himself out of thirty years of business.

Before I started working with Citrus World, I had been on the Conwood Smokeless Tobacco account, the largest division of Conwood Corporation, a company based in Memphis. Ted Powell, a former big New York agency guy who had gone to work for the client, was the VP of marketing and led a team of three product managers. Every young account executive in the ad business envied this kind of account. It was a large, national, consumer-directed piece of business with fifteen different brands covering three categories and encompassing almost every aspect of the ad business. TV, radio, print, outdoor, trade, in-store, and consumer promotion, and even event marketing, like NASCAR and more, were all being used. But more importantly, Ted taught me the value of really immersing myself in the client's business to determine how to best apply these promotional strategies in building their brands. He stressed the importance of direct involvement through in-market store checks, new product research, and participation in the development of yearly marketing plans. And yes, the job also meant learning how to chew, dip, spit, and even sniff tobacco! I was learning a lot working with Conwood, and we had a great relationship. But this was around the time that the government began to mandate the way tobacco companies did business. The government not only wanted health warnings on packages of smokeless tobacco, but they also placed regulations on all forms of advertising and completely banned the use of broadcast media.[1] The agency sadly decided it was best for both parties to end their long-time partnership due to the increased risk of legal liabilities. This was going to leave me without a major piece of business to work on. And I needed something. Little did I know how much of this first experience would shape my future with Walt.

•   •   •

Syl was now entrenched in the ad business. But this had never been his goal. In college, he studied math and science and thought he would be an architect. He had joined the agency just by chance.

SYL

I initially got into advertising in a very roundabout way. In college, I had been working toward a career in architecture. But the problem was I really didn't want to spend the additional years required to make this happen. During my last semester, the career counselors tried to sell me on the new exciting field of data processing. They thought they could convince me that this was where my best opportunities were. I thought about it—I even went to interviews with IBM and Honeywell. But I guess my two-toned wing tips weren't shined properly or my

---

1 *Wikipedia*, s.v. "Tobacco Advertising," accessed June 30, 2016. Last modified March 16, 2017
https://en.wikipedia.org/wiki/Tobacco_advertising

dark-blue suit was the wrong cut or my hair must have been way too long because I was soon able to rule those out. Next, the counselors pointed me to Nebraska, where I was going to interview to become an air-traffic controller.

One night, I was drinking with friends at my fraternity, and the later the evening got, the more I wondered aloud, "What the hell am I doing even thinking about going to Nebraska?" That was a legitimate question—I just couldn't imagine moving there.

One of my frat brothers asked me whether I'd ever thought about working for an ad agency. He knew that my girlfriend's neighbor in Atlanta was in charge of something called print production at an agency called Tucker Wayne & Company. I had no idea what print production was, but I thought it couldn't hurt to check it out. I needed a job!

And that's how I came to meet Jim Foster, who got me into this business. We just hit it off immediately. Jim was so patient and knowledgeable. He explained to me that working in print production was a great way to get started in the agency business. The agency was looking to hire young, ambitious people whom they could rotate through all the departments and mold into the perfect agency employees—ones who understood all the aspects of the business. I was to be the guinea pig for this program.

I graduated college on June 1, and by June 3, I was sitting at my desk, starting work.

On paper, the grand plan sounded better than it actually turned out to be. I thought I'd be moving faster, but I ended up staying in print production for four years. But beyond production, I learned about every aspect of the agency—creative, account service, media, and even some accounting. I was ready to broaden my skills. I learned that account service was where I wanted to be, and when I was ready to move out of production, I even interviewed in New York and Chicago. But Knox convinced me not to go and offered me an account-executive position reporting directly to him. I started out on accounts like Conwood Corporation, Flowers Industries, and Reynolds Metal.

When the agency resigned the Conwood account, I wasn't really sure what the future held for me.

It wasn't too long before I had my first new business pitch though. We won the GoodMark Foods account and partnered with them for the next three years. Unfortunately, soon after they went public, we parted ways. So, once again, I was faced with a questionable future.

It was around this time that the agency won the Citrus World account.

WALT

When we started working with Tucker Wayne, they mostly handled Donald Duck, which was our flagship brand at the time. We were so closely tied in to the duck that we had Donald on our water tower at the plant and had a huge figure of Donald Duck at the visitor's center. Inside were all kinds of Disney-licensed Donald Duck items and a video that showed how we processed the juice. Featured in the video was, who else? Donald Duck. So, at the time, this brand was our primary focus.

I had been charged with creating a brand, but in the meantime, we had juice to sell.

Once we joined forces with the new advertising agency, the first account team immediately began designing and placing Donald Duck orange-juice ads for us. They were gung ho. We had a guy who was pretty seasoned and a young, ambitious assistant. At some point, fairly early in the relationship, we ordered a high-value Donald Duck coupon ad to run in the newspapers in a Texas market. We anticipated a big response from the consumers. We had advised our customers in the market to stock up on our juice because the coupon offered a great deal, and we knew we would be moving lots of it.

On the Sunday the ad was supposed to run, I got a call from one of the category managers. He said, "What the hell am I going to do with all this juice?"

"What do you mean?" I told him. "There was a coupon. You're going to sell it!"

"There is no coupon in any newspaper down here," I heard back. I hung up the phone and called up our account guy, who immediately pushed it off to his assistant.

"The paper didn't run it!" he told me.

"Did you send them the order?" I demanded.

"Yes, absolutely! I'll call them right now and see what happened."

Well, we found out that the order was never sent in. The paper didn't run it because the paper never got the ad. I got a call back from the account assistant, who told me that he had spoken to a guy at the paper who said the paper made a mistake. They'd forgotten to run the ad. Meanwhile, we had our people in Texas call the paper, and they learned that they had never even been contacted by the agency.

One of my tenets is "Everyone makes mistakes, but don't lie to me." Our relationship was not off to the best start. And worse—the agency had embarrassed me.

I'm the kind of guy who might forgive, but I never forget. I waited to get even and soon found my chance.

A short while later, I was down in Cancun with the sales staff for our annual sales meeting. The agency guys came along. They were supposed to be presenting some new packaging work, which was four months overdue. The night they got there, they stayed out late drinking with the sales guys. So, I scheduled a meeting for six thirty the next morning for them to present their work. They were hungover, and the work was crap. It was obviously something they had just thrown together at the last minute.

I told them we were going out to a great club some of the guys had found called Club 21. I mentioned it was a sort of Mexican disco and that all the guys were going. After dinner, we went out and lined up for taxis to take us to this club. When the first one pulled up, I ushered the two agency guys inside and told them that we would be right behind. In my limited Spanish, I told the driver, "Club Veintiuno."

This place called itself a club. It was a local brothel. It got its name because it is twenty-one kilometers from the center of town. It was out in the middle of nowhere, in the jungle, and there was no one to turn to if you wanted to get out. Somehow, the agency guys made it home, and the next day, they tried to pretend that it had been great fun, the exact thing they had been looking for, and that it was too bad that we hadn't made it out there. But they couldn't keep up the charade for too long, especially when they were telling us one of the girls even followed them into the men's room to see if she could "help" them. They knew they had been set up. It was a little piece of get even for these two.

When we got back to the office, I called Knox and told him things weren't working out and that we needed a change. Knox talked me into staying with the agency, and that's when we got Syl. He was the definition of detail, follow-up, and service—a complete turnaround from what we had had. But I couldn't let him know that.

• • •

The contrast between Syl and the previous account supervisor was immediately palpable. Where the first guy was all flash and smoke, Syl was follow-up and detail. His background had taught him how to dig deeply into his clients' businesses and to anticipate next steps. He immediately took ownership of his position and dove into the orange-juice business by listening and learning, not by posturing and proclaiming.

SYL

Shortly after Walt complained about the first account team, I was brought in. Knox told me I had six months to straighten out the account, but it was really six months to save the Citrus World business. I got right to work.

I was able to get the train back on the track, but I was having a hard time getting close to Walt. It seemed that he had a built-in mistrust of the agency and always thought we were trying to take advantage of him and his budget. My first challenge was to clean up the mess that the other team had left behind.

At the midyear sales meeting, Walt decided that he needed us to develop and print an ad sheet for a Donald Duck promotion and deliver it to the meeting in Hilton Head in two days. Back then, that was a huge request. The ad needed to be designed, drawn, set into type, made into a mechanical layout, offset printed, dried, packed, and delivered. Today, you could do it on a laptop, push a button, and send it to a printer. In the 1980s, things were much more complicated.

I did the mental time calculations and tried not to panic as I talked to Walt, but when I hung up the phone, I thought, "There's no way."

An account exec often finds himself in the middle of a skirmish between the client and the creative department. I knew my biggest job would be to find a team that could work on this pronto and crank out a finished product in less than no time. So, I started with our creative director, Les Parker.

"I need a Donald Duck promotional ad! We have to deliver it to Hilton Head while the sales meeting is still on. We have only two days to get it to the client. I'm trying to do everything I can to get this guy on board with us, but I don't know how we are going to pull this off."

Les was the picture of calm. Tall, with oversized glasses and a big easy grin, he never seemed ruffled. Oh, he would tell you if you were overstepping, but he always tried to make things seem possible. And boy, was he talented. He was the perfect place to start.

Les calmed me down and called in our top writer. The two of them were composed and steady—and experienced in dealing with client emergencies. Together, they sat me down and said, "Let's get this done." In about an hour, the ad sheet was finished. Shortly after that, it was approved and in production. I still don't know how we finished it, but we got it printed, dried, and packed, and we rushed it off to the airport in time to make the last flight to Hilton Head.

Walt got the package, said "Thanks," and that was that. I found out later that he didn't even want the ad. It was a total test to see how high I could jump. I guess it worked. I stayed with them for twenty-seven years.

Syl's first sales sheet, which was a test from Walt.

3

Assembling a Team

I t was a struggle to get the Citrus World sales force up and running in an effective way. The company was moving in a new direction and Walt had to find a way to motivate this group, which was long used to working at an easy, predictable pace.

WALT

Out of the group of sales people I inherited, most were not worth keeping. But there was one jewel in the group—John Clarke—the private-label sales manager. John was from Polk County and quite a good ole character. He was young, funny, and willing to do whatever it took to move things ahead. John was very disarming. He appeared easygoing but could be hard as steel. With a sure quick wit and a strategic mind, he turned out to be my perfect alter ego.

John's friends called him "Hog Man." There is lots of conjecture about how he earned that moniker, which I won't go into here. On John's fortieth birthday, the sales force got

27

together and put a full-page ad in the *Winter Haven News Chief*. It said "Happy Birthday, Hog Man!" and it showed John balancing a spoon on the end of his nose with a big grin. Everyone loved John and he became a key element in my new strategies. If I was planning, he was execution. I started to lean on him.

One day, our CEO went to lunch with a salesperson and a customer. The salesperson showed zero aptitude for manners and had terrible table etiquette. The CEO came to me and said, "Walt, we have to get this fixed. This person will be traveling and meeting customers, and this behavior is embarrassing."

"Geez, how am I going to handle this?" I thought. "I know. We'll have a training session at the annual sales meeting to go over etiquette with everyone." Using a professional video, we covered things like which fork to use and that you should also pass the pepper when someone asks for the salt, things like that. Then came the part that would be entertaining while it drove the point home. People—especially salespeople—learn best when something is fun. I had asked John Clarke to find two women we could use to illustrate proper dress. So, he went down to a club on the strip in Orlando and brought back two entertainers who were willing to help us. One was supposed to dress in a cheap and suggestive way, and the other was to be a good example of business attire—modest clothing, stockings, and nice shoes. Well, the first one came out and paraded through the room. Everyone got a good laugh since her skimpy clothes obviously showed that she was a model of what not to wear. But then the second one came out, and she was trashier than the first! She was wearing a low-cut shirt, a short-short skirt, and high heels. She was an even bigger hit. "John!" I said. "I thought you were going to tell the second one to dress in office clothes."

"Well," said John, who by that time was pretty well into the scotch, "those girls brought in all these cute outfits, and that's what she wanted to wear. I couldn't make her wear those awful clothes."

So, that's what I was dealing with. But John quickly proved himself to be a good partner and a strong leader of the sales force. He understood people. And he could figure out when it was time to change tactics.

• • •

To the outside observer, John was the perfect foil for Walt. John ran interference with the customers and the sales force, often smoothing out the rough edges as Walt blazed a path.

Craig Steensen, Citrus World's Northeast at-home sales manager often observed their different tactics. As Craig recalls, "Walt and John meshed different personal styles to form a cohesive leadership team. Walt made quick judgments, often telling John, 'Of course, when you communicate this, you'll word it differently, right?' And John always did."

WALT

As John and I began working together, the two of us came up with a strategy for hiring the new generation of Citrus World salespeople. We figured out that we should get the most aggressive salespeople we could find who were motivated, young, and ambitious. But we soon found out that the people who fit this description weren't always the best team players. Let's just say we made some mistakes.

Early on, we had an opening for a regional manager in Pittsburgh. John found a guy whom we'll call Bill. His previous employers gave Bill a wonderful endorsement. They told us he was very aggressive and a real go-getter. John trained him at our office in Florida and then sent him off to his market. He fired him ten days later. Apparently, Bill had gone back to Pittsburgh, checked into a hotel, ordered up some beer and adult films, and tried to borrow money from our brokers when he ran out of cash. John and I realized that maybe character was as important as the level of aggressiveness.

Another guy on the sales force in the early days seemed to be unstoppable. He had great numbers and a thriving business. It wasn't until he tried to convince me that he could be in two places at one time that I figured all was not as it seemed.

In those days, salespeople kept track of their time through their sales reports. Credit-card receipts matched up to phone cards to show what the salesperson was doing. Occasionally, I did an audit to check the reports to be sure all was legit. I used methods from my days at Lever Brothers. Well, one day, I was looking over an expense report submitted by this guy, and I realized that the numbers were off. He had cheated and then tried to convince me that he had actually been in one place making a phone call and in another town taking a client out to dinner. I went out to his territory to fire him, but he was a pretty good salesman. I still can't believe it, but I was convinced he actually *was* in two places at once.

Soon after that, John Clarke took over as sales manager. Luckily for the company, John wasn't so easily fooled. Shortly after this salesman weaseled his way out of getting fired by me, he came to John and asked whether he and his wife could take a reward trip to Brazil the next day. We had been running an incentive program, and one of our distributors had won two tickets for a luxury trip. This sales guy tried to tell John that the customer who had won suddenly couldn't go and that since it would be a shame to waste the tickets, it would be better for him and his wife to take them. John hesitantly okayed it, but then we soon realized that this scheme had been planned. At that time, you needed a visa for travel to Brazil. There was no way the salesman could have pulled off a last-minute trip without some long-range planning. John figured it out and started watching him more closely. John told the salesman, "You fooled me once. There won't be a second time."

A couple of months later, this same salesman wanted to sponsor a golf tournament in his home territory. I told him no, because there was nothing Citrus World would have gained from it. It turned out that after I said no, he asked the broker to give him money for the tournament by submitting falsified invoices to the company for products and promotions. But the broker was more scared of John than of the salesman. He called John when his guilty conscience got to him. That was the end of our relationship with that salesman.

There's a famous saying from John Wooden, a former basketball Hall of Fame player and coach. He said, "Don't confuse activity with achievement." The problem with that salesman was that he always had lots of things going on. But he was also productive, so it was hard to see where the problems were. He brought me to another realization—that integrity is as important as sales skills.

I went back to basics again. I had to get our group in shape so people would take us seriously. Lever Brothers had many shortcomings, but they were professional, and for the first few years, I simply followed their systems. And to the locals, I looked like a genius. I began with basic training on how to sell. Using the Lever sales training manuals, I conducted sessions on basics like nonverbal communication and the three steps of a sales presentation: conditioning, proposal, and agreement—all basic stuff but revolutionary to our group. These had been just a bunch of guys with desks and telephones. We had sales meetings for the first time. I always tried to make them entertaining and fun. And slowly, we made some progress. I got rid of a bunch of people and recruited new ones, and we started to move forward.

In the early years, my idea was to engage the salespeople by letting them have fun whenever they could. We worked in a loose climate, with lots of joking and lots of testosterone-laden remarks flying around. But even though I gave those guys a lot of leeway, I still made sure they knew the boundaries. If I saw them having a bit too much late-night fun, I made sure to call an early-morning staff meeting that perhaps made them regret that raucous last call from the night before. I can still remember a meeting at which one sales manager had had too good a time. She was supposed to make a presentation to the whole group in the morning session. When I called for her to come up, she wasn't there. I asked, "Where is she?"

A voice from the back of the room said, "She's in the restroom throwing up."

Walt with members of the early sales force

Once, a major customer from New York City visited Citrus World. He didn't play golf, but he loved to fish and drink—a perfect match with one of our sales guys. Instead of staying at the hotel, the buyer opted to stay at the salesman's house. Apparently, they took advantage of being away from the office to party pretty hard the night before our meeting.

The plan for the day was that they would fish in the morning and then have a brief business review back at the office and then a plant tour. But our guy and the New York customer never showed up. They had started drinking early the previous afternoon, and the buyer had fallen asleep in the bathtub! I guess we were lucky he didn't fall off the boat and drown.

Once at a sales meeting, this same sales guy ran out of money. He started calling random phone numbers in the hotel, trying to find someone he knew. He finally landed on our VP of sales, who had been sound asleep. Well, it was two o'clock in the morning. Our VP got up, stumbled around, and still remembers getting lost in the closet because he was so disoriented from the late-night phone call. The truth is he was probably sleeping it off himself.

I bring these stories up to show what a different time and place it was. We had very few women working in the sales department, and all of our guys had a lot of freedom. They were encouraged to have fun and get along with each other—as long as they got their jobs done.

● ● ●

But then came the Clarence Thomas era. Sexual misbehavior, crudely suggestive talk, and a lax attitude toward both were in the national spotlight. The new world of business did not tolerate hostile workplaces. Suddenly, corporate culture had to tone it down, to straighten up. And it came at a good time for our team. They still had fun, but there were some things that could not be condoned anymore.

The structure Walt had put into place in the early years led to transformation in the sales organization. Although they behaved like fraternity brothers at times, the salesmen—for a long while, there were only men on the team—knew what was expected of them. And when the rules toward acceptable behavior began to change, they knew how to respond.

WALT

We still liked to have our fun, but the sales force had come a thousand miles from where it was when we first started. We were now a professional group, interested in learning together and supporting each other and taking pride in our combined achievements.

A major tangible way that the sales force had changed was the fact that it was now a diverse group. During my tenure, we hired the first black sales manager, the first woman, and the first Hispanic person. And those firsts were soon joined by others.

For instance, one woman, Mandy Hancock, joined the company at the lowest entry-level sales position. She quickly rose through the ranks to become the first female director-level manager. Mandy combined a strong intellect, a hard work ethic, and a natural business sense. She was an invaluable asset to our team—and a sign that our team was moving forward.

SYL

Once the sales department started expanding to include women, the group became more professional. But even though the outrageous behavior was toned down, a lot of the fun elements still came at the sales meetings. Walt was a big believer in team building. We packed every meeting with group activities, like boat- and car-building competitions, paintball games, beach Olympics events, game shows, murder mysteries, talent shows—you name it.

One midyear sales meeting was held at Hilton Head, South Carolina. It's a great place for a group to gather, but in the spring, the weather is not as predictable as it is in Florida. Hilton Head is well known for its golf courses, and our big activity was to be a golf tournament. Well, unfortunately, it snowed the day we got out there. The agency had brought along a photographer to get some shots of the teams. The agency's big idea was to rush away from the course, get the slides developed, and then surprise the group by showing them at the banquet that night. This is another thing that would be no big deal today since you can show photos instantly. But at the time, it was a bit challenging to rush off the island, find a way to process the slides, and make an instant presentation. To top it all off, most of the shots were of our sales team covered from head to toe in all the extra clothing they had brought with them. They were wrapped in sweaters, hats, and even towels as the snow fell down on them. But not one person quit or even walked off the course for a break. And they loved the presentation—the slides flashed by to the tune of "Don't Worry, Be Happy."

At least at that meeting, there were no casualties. Once when we played a game of friendly softball together, someone took a ball to the eye, which broke his glasses and gave him a nice cut on his cheekbone. Another time, two of our senior—and fleshier—sales guys challenged each other to a foot race. We all lined up on the sidelines, chanting for our favorite contender. About twenty yards in, one of them pulled a muscle, while the other fell to the ground clutching his chest. We thought that he was having a heart attack! Eventually, they both got up and staggered away.

WALT

I remember the murder mystery. I had assigned each salesperson to assume the role of a famous person in history. We had generals, cartoon characters, and statesmen. John and I had fun picking the historical characters. We used the criteria of physical appearance, job function, or personality to make the selections, matching the salesperson to a relevant historical character. For instance, we had General Lee and General Grant and even Lenin and Stalin. One female sales manager from the South, who was affectionately called the Debutante, was assigned the role of Clara Barton. But the Debutante vehemently objected and instead opted to be Mata Hari, complete with an iconic sexy outfit.

It took a while, but John and I created a professional, dedicated sales force that was team oriented. A big advantage we had over our competitors was the fact that our sales force only sold juices, so we became experts. Our customers relied on our team for market and crop information. Turnover and reorganization at our competitors' businesses meant they had no real knowledge of the commodity aspect of citrus juices. Even though we were the smallest of the companies, on more than a few occasions, we were the market leaders on commodity pricing changes. Simply put, our competitors had no idea what was happening in the groves on a timely basis.

4

Eureka!

By 1985, Citrus World had come a long way toward building a solid program. The sales staff was more organized and focused, and it was following a plan. The production facilities were being updated and were cranking out a record number of cases of juice each week.

But in spite of all of this forward motion, the cooperative still wanted to move away from its private label and Donald Duck history. For a time, the marketing team focused on Donald Duck's frozen concentrate that was packaged as a juice block, a square package that was easy to open and easy to stack in the freezer. In focus groups and in testing, consumers agreed that the package was more environmentally friendly and easier to use, and it took up less space in the freezer than the traditional round cans. This was Walt's first lesson in realizing that attitudes do not predict behavior. In spite of the good response, the juice block was slow to catch on, and even with promotions, contests, and giveaways, it never gained traction. The situation in the market was that frozen concentrate was no longer a growth category. It had been developed during World War II when the War Department wanted to send more nutritious foods to the troops. To the soldiers in the trenches, orange juice was a taste of home. Starting with Birdseye in the 1950s and through the 1960s and 1970s, frozen concentrate was a convenient alternative to fresh-squeezed juice—with just a bit of water and stirring, housewives could be ready for the breakfast rush in no time at all. But by the 1980s, ready-to-serve juice had become more widely available, and it seemed as if the market was ready to move in that direction.

The business of selling orange juice had begun to grow and change in 1954 when orange-juice pioneer Anthony Rossi developed a new method for processing fresh juice. This technique was called flash pasteurization, and it resulted in a means of maintaining the flavor of ready-to-serve juice under refrigeration. This meant that the chilled product could be mass marketed for the first time. Packed in wax cartons and glass bottles, it was distributed in many locations across the country. The strongest market for this orange juice was New York City, which was dominated by Tropicana. They called their ready-to-serve juice Pure Premium. It was different—this one was not from concentrate.

Tropicana offered orange juice that tasted freshly squeezed to the mass market. Although other processors were not equipped to produce juice that was not from concentrate, some took notice and tried to answer this challenge in a roundabout way.

Minute Maid was one of them. Long a powerhouse in the frozen-concentrate category, it also competed in the chilled category with juice packaged in the distinctive black carton. This offered the convenience of ready-to-serve juice in a from-concentrate form. Rather than jumping into the not-from-concentrate market, they competed by claiming that the concentrating process helped the taste of their juice since they could use a blend of oranges picked at their seasonal best, instead of relying only on one variety.[1]

For a time, Citrus World focused on its Donald Duck chilled from-concentrate product, which it sold successfully in several regions across the country. But the freight cost for shipping product that was reconstituted (i.e., full of water) was much higher than that for shipping concentrate. So, by 1986, Citrus World had two plants, one in Winston-Salem, North Carolina, and one in Fullerton, California. These facilities produced and packed Donald Duck chilled juice. As regional packers and shippers, they could more economically cover chilled-juice markets across the country. Now, they just had to get the product sold into the stores.

WALT

We had tried to sell our from-concentrate Donald Duck to Winn-Dixie, a major Southeastern grocery chain, many times without success. Other retailers we had met with would politely, and sometimes impolitely, turn us down. So, I came

---

1 "The Minute Maid Company History," in *History of The Minute Maid Company—FundingUniverse*; "Orange Juice Wars Began in 1973," in *History of The Minute Maid Company—FundingUniverse*; accessed July 7, 2016. http://www.fundinguniverse.com/company-histories/the-minute-maid-company-history/

up with a brilliant and innovative idea to convince Winn-Dixie to take the product. I would give it to them *free*. Now, who turns down something that is free?

Our broker in Miami, Herb Bell, was the prototypical food broker. He was the master at walking the fine line between the manufacturers, who paid him, and the buyers, who controlled the grocery shelves. Herb had a great relationship with all the buyers.

Winn-Dixie Miami was a huge buyer of chilled juice. Tropicana was their number-one-selling brand. Herb knew the buyer well. Herb and I went to call on him together. I proposed to the buyer that we would give him two *free* truckloads of Donald Duck chilled juice, just to get it in his store and to show that it would sell. After this trial, I was sure Winn-Dixie would carry it in its stores.

The buyer wouldn't even let me finish my pitch. He said two things: "no" and "don't come back!"

• • •

The orange-juice category had matured since the intro-duction of from-concentrate juice. Thanks to Tropicana, consumers were beginning to be educated about chilled not-from-concentrate juices. Tropicana had spent lots of money advertising its brand, essentially paving the way for new product introductions. Consumers were more sophisticated and had become aware of the taste difference in chilled—even chilled concentrate—versus canned or frozen juices. And growing demand showed they were willing to pay more. As incomes in the United States grew and lives became more complicated, consumers opted for convenience and fresher products. Chilled juice filled both of those orders since it was ready made. What's more, not-from-concentrate juice offered the closest taste to that of freshly squeezed.

But although the market was ready, finances were always a major consideration for Citrus World. Obligations to the grower-owners and the expense of taking on new products and processes made expansion decisions difficult, especially since entering the chilled-juice market would mean competing with Minute Maid and Tropicana. Their deep pockets were intimidating, at the very least. Nonetheless, it was time to do something.

WALT

Herb and I talked the situation over on the way back to the Miami airport. I was flying home, defeated. Herb made a throwaway comment, "Why don't we make a premium juice like Tropicana?"

HERB BELL, FOOD BROKER

After our meeting at Winn-Dixie, Walt and I knew that we couldn't make a chilled from-concentrate Donald Duck juice work in our market.

I casually tossed out the idea that we had to do something totally different and come up with a pure not-from-concentrate premium juice to really give the consumers what they wanted.

Walt immediately dismissed this idea and spent the rest of the drive telling me that this just couldn't be done. It would cost too much to set it up. It would be too hard to supply the market on a year-round basis. There was no system for preparing and holding the juice in the off-season.

Well, he convinced me. Premium juice just couldn't be done at Citrus World. By the time I dropped him off at the airport, I thought I'd never hear from him again about a not-from-concentrate juice option.

WALT

On the plane home, I suddenly thought, "Damn! We *have* to do this!" All of the reasons *not* to do it were the very reasons to do it! All the barriers to entry made it more attractive. It wasn't a crowded category, and if we could figure out how to make it work before others jumped in, we would have an advantage. And the trade needed another brand to add competition in the fast-growing not-from-concentrate segment.

HERB

A couple of days later, Walt called me like a raving wild man and said I had a couple of hours to get him pricing on premium juice. So, I knew he was serious.[2]

WALT

I went back to management with this new product idea and heard first from our then VP of sales. He assured me it would never work and that it would cost too much to produce.

---

2 Susan Spann, *The History of Florida's Natural*, 1995, promotional video.

But CEO Joe Marshburn, ever the entrepreneur, backed the project.

I put together a new proposal, and Herb went back to the Winn-Dixie buyer. This time, Herb only took with him a black-and-white line drawing of the new product. The buyer bought it immediately. It's not that Winn-Dixie was that interested in our new not-from-concentrate juice, since we didn't even have a sample. They were very interested in developing some competition for Tropicana. They shrewdly knew that our entry into the market would make Tropicana bring more promotional money to the retailers.

• • •

Dan McSpadden, Citrus World's director of marketing, talked about how unique this new premium juice product was. He said, "Sometimes, new product ideas are handed down from the research department. But this new not from concentrate was born in the field. It was market driven. The consumers wanted it."[3]

Deciding to go ahead with the product was just the first step. Walt had to convince the board that this was the way to go. He reminded them that he had been hired to create a brand for the company. They thought it would be a Donald Duck chilled from-concentrate product, but he convinced them that

---

[3] Dan McSpadden, telephone interview, in discussion with the author, February 23, 2016. Quotes from Dan McSpadden used throughout the book come from the same interview.

that was not the right direction. He showed them the research, outlined a plan, and told them his team had buyers lined up. They sanctioned him to proceed.

Ideas for new brand entries are easy. Actually executing the idea is daunting. Citrus World had a plant designed to make canned juice and concentrate and very little of what it needed to produce not-from-concentrate juice. Before anything else was done, the company had to answer the question of how to have a year-round supply of juice since fresh oranges were only available about six months out of the year.

WALT

Bob Williard is a food scientist and was our VP of technical services. Anything concerning flavor, taste, or processing was in his area. He ran the quality-control department and the research-and-development lab, and he directed the packing process to be sure product quality was maintained. I was talking to him one day about the new product idea and told him our biggest problem was storing juice for the off-season. If this product took off like I hoped it would, we would need to be storing tens of thousands of gallons of juice. Out of the blue, Bob said, "Why don't we store it in aseptic bags?"

I didn't know what he was talking about. We had aseptic packages—juice in our glass bottles was packaged aseptically, which was basically a method of sterilizing both the package and the juice, but I couldn't figure out how he planned to store a large quantity.

BOB WILLIARD, RETIRED VP OF TECHNICAL SERVICES, CITRUS WORLD

I'd like to say that the package for our new premium juice was the result of many years of research and technology. But the truth is that Citrus World had already been using aseptic packages for a couple of its products. Plus, what Walt didn't know was that we had just completed a study of citrus juice packed in small plastic bags. It wasn't for any particular project—we just thought we might be able to use it someday. We had tested the taste and freshness of the juice packed this way and figured it was a process worth trying.

WALT

We started working on making huge aseptic bags that could hold three hundred gallons of juice. These were packed into wooden boxes under multiple layers of foil and stored in a refrigerated warehouse. Next, we had to be sure this system was going to work and that the juice was going to stay fresh. Again, Bob came up with an ingenious solution. I asked him, "Has anyone ever packed three hundred gallons of aseptic orange juice?" To say that I was worried about this is an understatement.

His answer was less than reassuring. "I've done dozens of one-gallon bags. Should work."

BOB

The next job was to stack the wooden crates with the bags of juice in the warehouse. At the top of each bag, we attached a little balloon filled with red dye. When juice spoils, it expands, so we figured that any spoiling juice would push outward against the balloon, causing it to ooze red dye. We sent company inspectors crawling around the warehouse with flashlights at all hours of the night and day, looking for that telltale red ooze.

WALT

We made three thousand bins of juice and prayed.

BOB

Spoilage was never detected so we knew we could store enough juice to cover customer demands during the off-season.[4]

• • •

Citrus World sales manager John Clarke vouches for the significance of this successful experiment. "We knew we had a good product, but figuring out how to store it was a major roadblock. Once we tested Bob Williard's packaging and saw that it worked—that's when we knew that maybe this could actually happen."[5] Citrus World was on its way to making premium juice. It would be called Fresh'N'Natural.

---

4 Susan Spann, *The History of Florida's Natural*, 1995, promotional video.

5 John Clarke, telephone interview, in discussion with the author, March 2, 2016. Quotes from John Clarke used throughout the book come from the same interview.

WALT

Without Bob's idea, Citrus World would never have had a brand. This juice-storing technology got us going. It's interesting that Tropicana, which had a huge infrastructure to store its juice in huge frozen blocks, completely converted to aseptic tanks after our entry into the market.

A few years later, we began using refrigerated aseptic tank farms instead, which was another step forward for us. We had lots of warehouse space since we had been storing canned juice for years. We easily converted this to refrigerated warehouse space to store the tens of thousands of bins we eventually needed.

• • •

The story so far: The market was changing, and Citrus World had to catch up to stay in the game. Walt picked up an off-hand remark from a broker and decided to push for a not-from-concentrate premium orange-juice brand. Local markets accepted the idea, and the Citrus World board approved.

Concerns turned to practical matters—processing and storing. A new technique allowed Citrus World to overcome this hurdle.

With that groundwork laid, the next big issue was the package.

WALT

International Paper provided the carton packaging for our company and for all of our competitors. International Paper's products were high quality, and we had a great relationship with them. But since they packed for Tropicana, I didn't want to risk Tropicana finding out we were working on a new product that would compete with theirs. We had a buying co-op named HESCO that purchased all of our packing supplies. I called Gap Kovach, HESCO's president.

GAP KOVACH, HESCO PRESIDENT

Walt called and told me about the new product. He said he needed my help. He wanted superior graphics with excellent carrying qualities at an extremely good price. And he wanted it yesterday. Oh—and no one was to know a thing about it. All these stipulations tied my hands a bit.

WALT

Gap had worked for Citrus World for years, and his main job had been to purchase packaging materials, like corrugated boxes and paper labels. But now, we were looking for high-quality cartons with a new printing process. It was a reach for his company. But I knew Gap could work something out.

GAP

My staff and I devised a plan. With only two months to design, execute, print, pack, and ship the cartons, we got busy. I started by finding a place to print. EloPak, a European company that printed cartons, had a printing plant in Barbados. Yes, the tiny Caribbean island. I have no idea why. This was remote enough that Walt figured no one would ever know what we were doing.

Plus, when we looked into shipping charges from the island, we learned that it was very expensive to ship *to* Barbados, but since the vessels always returned to the United States empty, it would be very inexpensive to do the reverse route.

WALT

While Gap was working on logistics, the agency and I were coming up with the final packaging design and artwork. This carton was to be a departure from the old flexographic printing process, which was the standard for the industry. Flexo is cheap, but the graphics are poor due to the rubber plate used in printing. We had little money to advertise, so I decided that the package had to carry our message on its own. It needed to look better than the competitors' cartons. We were going to switch to rotogravure, which allowed us to use up to six colors and yielded a much higher-quality, more-appetizing-looking finished package. Rotogravure involved making engraved cylindrical plates after we had completed the final artwork. The package would have real taste appeal.

This was another place where our innovations changed the not-from-concentrate industry. After our entry and use of high-quality graphics, every major brand switched to high-quality graphic printing.

GAP

HESCO had the engraved metal plates shipped in from France. We got a trained press operator from England. We ordered special paper from Finland. The first batch of packages came out perfectly. It was all starting to come together, as Walt had scripted.

WALT

The first round of packages arrived at the Citrus World plant in Florida, and they were beautiful. Our packers filled them and we rolled out our new product into the Florida market. It was so well received that within a week, we were getting distribution and sales and reorders. It was obvious we would surpass our sales forecast.

So, I called Gap and matter-of-factly told him we needed the next load of cartons ASAP.

We were just up and running and already selling better than we had planned. There was no way we could miss delivery deadlines for our reorders or our new customers.

GAP

I was feeling cocky. After all, the first order had gone exactly as planned, so what could go wrong?

Well, as it turned out, plenty went wrong.

I called the Barbados plant and gave them the new order. They said it would be on the water in a week. It wasn't. Every day, Walt called and asked, "Where are my cartons?"

Suddenly, no one answered my calls at the plant in Barbados. Then, I called after six o'clock in the evening and got the plant cleanup crew, who matter-of-factly mentioned, "Oh, the side seamer is broken."

I reported the situation to Walt, who told me, "Go down there, and don't come back unless you have the cartons." I got to Barbados and found the cartons were all printed and cut but not folded and seamed. At that point, I was trying not to panic. I had no choice but to ship all the flat, printed cartons to the States for sealing. And though we were trying to keep our plans a secret, we had to ship them to International Paper, which packed for Tropicana.

Since we had been planning to ship fully formed cartons to Florida, we now had to scramble to figure out how to pack these flat cardboard forms for shipping to Atlanta, where International Paper was going to work on them. There are no twenty-four-hour stores in Barbados, and we had no supplies for shipping the unsealed cartons. Somehow, we came up with the materials to make shipping cases, and we made them by hand.

When we were done, we had forty thousand pounds of material to get to the airport. In Barbados, there are no superhighways, and not many small highways either. And there were no tractor-trailers. So, our crew commandeered fourteen or fifteen pickup trucks and caravanned off to the airport. When we got there, the plane, which was the last cargo flight for the day, was already full. Using some international diplomacy (i.e., money), we got the cargo handlers to empty the plane and put our shipment in.

We flew to Miami. A trailer waiting there took the cargo and me to Lake Wales. A new driver got behind the wheel, and we went on to Atlanta to seal the cartons, and then headed back to Lake Wales. We got there by four o'clock in the morning on Sunday, in time for packing and filling at seven. We did not miss a single order by even one day.

A couple of months later, Walt surprised me with a beautiful leather jacket that had the inscription *Indiana Kovach*.[6]

WALT

Let's just say that our new product introduction surprised Tropicana. And we surprised ourselves. In two months, with an ad budget of $5,000, we outsold every other brand in the market except Tropicana.

The first Fresh'N'Natural package

6 Susan Spann, *The History of Florida's Natural*, 1995, promotional video.

5

The Launch

When Fresh'N'Natural, entered the market in 1987, there were many other products on the refrigerated shelves. Chilled ready-to-serve from-concentrate juice was dominated by Minute Maid and private-label brands. And of course, Tropicana owned the premium not-from-concentrate market. Citrus World had to break in with a great product, but it had limited funds to promote it.

WALT

We came up with the Fresh'N'Natural name by employing a linguist in New York who conceived it for a new product that was to be jointly produced with another cooperative. But this never got off the ground, which left us with a name we had already paid for. Since the package would be the primary spokes piece, the name was perfect. It had to express the key attributes of the product. Once we decided to use it, we turned the name over to the agency to get the design going.

SYL

Walt had told the agency that the package had to sell the product. Chuck Mumah, an art director who worked on the account for many years, was involved from the very beginning. But the way he got the package artwork going became one of the moments Walt never let us forget.

Chuck had drawn a glass filled with orange juice with half of an upended orange suspended over it. Coming out of that orange was a drip that was heading for the glass. Well, Chuck and my predecessor somehow convinced Walt that the only guy in the world who could draw a perfect orange for them was in Japan. As Walt tells it, the cost was $20,000. (I learned later that the original cost was actually $14,000, but the reported cost rose each time Walt retold the story.)

WALT

I remember thinking, "Twenty thousand dollars! For an orange?" But I had hired the agency to be the experts, so I figured they knew what to do. I okayed it. And do you know what we got? An orange! Sure, it was a nice orange, but it was still just an orange! By the way, the agency got its 15 percent commission. Lesson learned. That's the last time I didn't go with my gut.

SYL

The creative team used that orange on the first package, and believe me, I lived with that story and Walt's rising cost details for twenty-seven years. And I hadn't even been involved!

WALT

I had a lot to learn. I didn't have much experience working with an ad agency, and I was still trying to figure out how to handle the players. I knew they were the experts and had more knowledge of packaging and print production than I did, but being the cost-cutting guy I had always been, I felt like I was always being upsold.

I remember getting on a plane in Atlanta once. I was actually flying to LA with the agency guys. We were heading out to shoot a commercial in California for the first—and it turns out the last—time. I headed over to my gate and saw the agency team huddled over at the ticket counter. The head of research came over to me and said, "Walt, good news. We got you upgraded to first class." Well, I knew that they were already flying in first and didn't want it to look bad.

"No, thanks," I said. "I like to fly coach." And on that trip, I guess they did too. At least they were smart enough to move back to where I was sitting. That's just one example of our different ideas on how to spend a client's money.

SYL

It was shortly after the product introduction that I came on the scene. By now, there were plenty of things Walt was steamed about. He thought filming an ad in California was an extravagant waste of money. He was upset about the Donald Duck ad that never ran in Texas. We were months late in delivering another product's new packaging recommendations. And then there was the dripping orange. I knew I had my work cut out for me.

WALT

When Knox made the personnel change and put Syl on the Citrus World account, it saved the business for them. We worked together for twenty-seven years. Our old account supervisor was full of empty promises. Syl was the consummate professional account guy. He served both the agency and his clients. And he followed up on every detail. At first, I thought, "Is this guy for real?" I wondered if he was just a yes-man. But he delivered every time and quickly proved he had a nimble intellect and the perfect temperament to balance the client and the agency.

In later years, Syl and I took lots of trips together. I would say, "We're all going to the Rio Negro."

Syl would say, "Great! By the way, where's the Rio Negro?" When we got back, he would say, "Where are we going next?" I wondered if he actually liked hanging out with me or if he was just trying to be the perfect account executive. But I don't think the agency paid for those trips for him, so that must have counted for something.

Syl sweating his way through the Brazilian jungle

The group assembled in the Brazilian rainforest. Syl and
Walt with Photographer Charlie McCullers, Art Director
Chuck Mumah, and Research Director Harry Vardis.

Charlie McCullers, Syl, and Walt in India

Walt and Chuck Mumah relaxing at camp in India

Explorers at break time. Walt and Syl with Chuck Mumah in India.

A stylish Syl on safari in Africa

Chuck Mumah on safari in Africa

Syl Trekking in the Himalayas

•   •   •

While Walt struggled with managing the agency, and Syl struggled with managing Walt, each worked to figure out the particulars of the shifting orange-juice marketplace.

At this point, there were lots of juice competitors in the chilled category. But the market for premium not-from-concentrate juice was still far from developed. A slide used in Citrus World's 2012 stockholder presentations showed that in 1987, only 8 percent of orange juice sold at the retail level was not from concentrate, and that was all Tropicana. On the other hand, 47 percent of what was sold was frozen; 44 percent was reconstituted, which was coming from Minute Maid, dairies, and private labels; and 1 percent was freshly squeezed.

The slide went up through the years to show how the market had changed. Over twenty years the market had shifted to 8 percent frozen and 52 percent not from concentrate—a complete flip. The companies that were selling only frozen are now out of business. So, of the companies selling orange juice when Citrus World jumped in, only a small handful remain today.

Cultural and economic shifts in the 1980s influenced shoppers' buying habits. Busy families with working mothers craved convenience. And since many consumers could afford to buy premium products, fresh taste moved up to a priority position.

Although there were many small competitors in the marketplace, Fresh'N'Natural, in a move that many might call naïve, had lined itself up to compete with some of the biggest names in the beverage business—Minute Maid and Tropicana. That was a gutsy move for a company with only $200 million in annual sales.

WALT

Many of the smaller competitors just couldn't make it in the business. They couldn't react quickly enough to changes and didn't have a brand-marketing approach. They were just trying to sell juice and didn't distinguish themselves from the others on the shelves. Citrus World was trying to sell juice, of course, but our overriding effort was to build a brand for the company. Without that focus, we would have been just another company packing juice.

One thing that amused me, in retrospect, was that a lot of other companies looked down on us. Granted, Citrus World's reputation over the years was not the best. It had some management problems, a weak balance sheet, and sales-force problems, and it was easy to see why the other companies had this attitude. When they saw what we were doing—introducing a premium not-from-concentrate product—some of them said, "If Citrus World can do this—it can't be that hard!" One guy from Lykes Pasco said he would double our sales. Well, Lykes Pasco is no longer a juice company, and newspaper reports from a few years ago described them as having made "a failed bid in the premium juice category."[1]

• • •

The Fresh'N'Natural introduction in Miami convinced Citrus World that they had to move forward quickly with a larger rollout. And they knew that they had to go head-to-head with Tropicana and enter the New York market.

JOE MARSHBURN, FORMER CEO, CITRUS WORLD

It was decision time. We had completed the Fresh'N'Natural market test in Miami and had to decide where to go from there. We knew that the major markets would be very expensive and

---

1 Chase Squires, "Pasco: Vitality Chairman Touts Future of Juice Business," *St. Petersburg Times*, June 13, 2000, accessed June 30, 2016. www.sptimes.com/News/061300/news_pf/Pasco/Vitality_chairman_tou.shtml

that we had to be extremely targeted. And after looking at our options, it was clear that we had to move into New York, followed by California. We presented this action plan to the board. It took several meetings—the expense and the immensity of the proposal really pushed the boundaries of what seemed prudent to our board members. But the management team convinced them that it was not a time for prudence, and they finally agreed that we should move ahead.[2]

WALT

Citrus World had to get a food broker in New York to represent Fresh'N'Natural at retail. It would be the broker's job to present our brand to the retail buyers.

One thing we learned pretty quickly is that the distance between Lake Wales and New York is a lot more than 1,200 miles. New Yorkers have a reputation for being rough and tumble, almost cutthroat. The grocery business is no different. And dealing with the brokers there is not like dealing with more reserved markets in the South. In New York, they are noisy, direct, and not long on pleasantries.

We didn't have anyone like that. But we did have John Clarke. We sent him to talk to Pezrow, our new broker in New York.

We couldn't have orchestrated this better. Those abrasive New York guys and Hog Man were worlds apart. But everyone likes John, and these people were no different.

_____

2 Susan Spann, *The History of Florida's Natural*, 1995, promotional video.

Years later, Pezrow broker Jerry Heller provided a tongue-in-cheek description of his first meeting with John Clarke.

JERRY HELLER, FOOD BROKER

We got a call that a small company in Florida wanted us to rep their orange juice. So, we set up a meeting with John Clarke.

While waiting for him to arrive at our office, the largest white limo I'd ever seen pulled up out front. And out came this portly man who looked like he hadn't missed a meal in a while. I look at the size of the limo and the size of him, and I thought to myself, "These guys have money. We're bringing them in!"

But then I got John into my office, and I started looking him over. I thought, "I'm not sure I like this guy yet. Look how he's dressed, like Arnold Palmer—polyester pants and funny-looking clothes. It isn't what we wear in New York."

John introduced himself to everybody—he came across as a laid-back redneck. Then he started talking, and nobody could understand what the heck he was saying. He started telling us about oranges and how we had to get to know our buyers. We had to work with them, take them out, and play golf with them. He thought working with a buyer in New York was like it was down South. What he didn't realize was that we didn't have time for all this shtick. If you brought a buyer outside in New York, he would kill you and take your money.

Anyway, it was a typical Friday meeting in New York. We were all talking at once, looking at our watches, and trying to wrap it up. But then someone brought up a subject that was important to us. We wanted to put the kosher symbol on the package, which is a *K* or a *U* inside a circle. John was trying to follow the conversation and was looking sort of lost. Finally, he stood up and announced to the room, "Look, y'all, if you want the whole damn alphabet on the carton, that's what we'll do!" Well, it took us a while to figure out what he'd said, and it actually gave us a great laugh. We told him we only needed the symbol on the package for the holidays.[3]

•   •   •

Just like the Winn-Dixie buyer at the start of the process, the New York brokers welcomed competition in the market. Little by little, everything started to come together. But there were still some hiccups along the way.

WALT

There were a few times when our production team faced packaging challenges. One of the most frustrating was when we tried to install the twist-and-seal pour spout on the gable of the carton. This was an innovation that no other not-from-concentrate package had, and if we got it out first, it would give us a real advantage in the category. The only problem was that we just couldn't get it to work right. The machinery wouldn't secure it to the package, and the machines kept shutting down during the process. Our competitors gave up on trying to install pour spouts because they were having production problems of their own.

---

3 Susan Spann, *The History of Florida's Natural*, 1995, promotional video.

We had a self-taught mechanic on the line—Bobby Westmoreland—and he took the pour spout on as his personal project. Bobby would sleep at the plant and get up in the middle of the night to keep the lines running. Or, he would go home and come back to check on things and fix them if necessary. This was the ultimate sacrifice for Bobby, whose real passion was fishing. The machine manufacturers couldn't fix the problem, and for a while, it looked like we had lost our chance to introduce this innovation. Bobby was a line mechanic, a country boy, who in another life would have been a mechanical engineer. He stuck with the problem and finally got it fixed. Ultimately, he created some innovations on the machinery that the manufacturer incorporated. We were finally able to run cartons. This gave us a real edge over our competitors.

Bobby exemplified the can-do spirit of the whole Citrus World company. Everyone at Citrus World had come to embrace the brand as his or her own. So many people contributed in big and small ways to make it grow.

• • •

Once the manufacturing, packaging, and distribution processes came together, it was time to roll out some advertising.

SYL

From the outset, budget drove our marketing plans, and we had to make sure our ads really delivered. When it came time to produce our first commercial to back up the New York rollout, we knew it was crucial to establish the product name and the package design in the consumers' minds. So, we came up with a strategy that incorporated the images and actions of the on-camera talent with the package graphics. For many consumers, this ad would be the first time they would be exposed to the new brand. Our technique was to use energetic music with song lyrics and visuals to mimic the package. We titled the commercial "Name Says It All." Our model was tall and blond. We had to dye her hair orange. We gave her green-striped pants and a flowing white shirt. She danced and tumbled as oranges rained down and rolled around her. It didn't take long for us to internally label our first Fresh'N'Natural commercial "Bouncing Bimbo."

Scenes from the "Name Says It All" commercial

That commercial helped establish the Fresh'N'Natural name in the marketplace, but it didn't help that much in selling product. It didn't really stand for anything. It was mostly a thirty-second piece of entertainment. We decided we had to focus on a particular aspect of the juice and target our biggest competitor, Tropicana.

WALT

The "Bouncing Bimbo" spot was only valuable in showing us what *not* to do.

SYL

With our researchers we launched a taste test in New York. The test was conducted in various locations throughout the metropolitan area. We did a head-to-head comparison of Fresh'N'Natural and Tropicana. And we won.

Around the time of the taste tests, we also found out that Tropicana, at different times of the year, sometimes froze some of their not-from-concentrate juice and then mixed it back into the product before packaging. We presented that information in our ad, a commercial called "Cold Facts," which was illustrated by a frozen orange ball that got plunked down next to the Tropicana carton. Then we mentioned the results of the taste test. Consumers put the two facts together, and we were off and running. The campaign ended with a 6 percent sales increase against a 6 percent price increase. That commercial, with our claim that Fresh'N'Natural was never frozen, got Tropicana's attention fast.

Citrus World then began expanding the brand geographically into Chicago and Southern California.

After that, we illustrated the difference between our brand and Tropicana with a commercial called "Stripping Cartons." Again, since budget was always a consideration for us, this one was relatively inexpensive to produce. We showed two cartons, side by side, one Fresh'N'Natural and one Tropicana. Removing one element at a time, we stripped the cartons bare, saying, "Take away the name; take away the graphics," until all that was left were blank cartons. Then we talked about the taste test results and brought the Fresh'N'Natural visuals back up. It was direct, and it was unmistakably shaking a hornet's nest. We felt there was nothing to be worried about. After all, everything we said was *true*.

6

The Lawsuits

WALT

Well, everything our advertising said may have been true, but the big company didn't like it. In the spring of 1987, we were hit with our first lawsuit, just as our packages were appearing in the market. Our competitor didn't like that our package claimed our product was fresh.

This was the start of busy times for our general counsel, David Latham. David is smart, with a sharp South African wit. He has a great way of boiling cloudy issues down to a clear broth, and when our troubles started to complicate things, he knew how to defend the company's position. He understood that we had limited resources and had to make each advertising message and each design element count, so he got moving on our behalf. This lawsuit was just a reaction to our being in the marketplace at all. The competition wanted us out. It was a case of the big guy trying to rub out the pesky newcomer using money and the cost of litigation to do it.

DAVID LATHAM, CITRUS WORLD ATTORNEY

Apparently, the big orange juice company didn't want the monopoly broken up, so they sued Citrus World. Remember, they were the only real players in the not-from-concentrate category. They claimed we shouldn't be using the word *fresh* on the label, but we disagreed. And the judge agreed with us. And he was upheld on appeal.

• • •

And then came the second commercial: "Cold Facts."

DAVID

This time, Tropicana didn't like our advertising. We claimed our juice tasted more like fresh squeezed than theirs. We said they sometimes froze their juice. And to show it, we used a frozen ball of orange juice. Well, they didn't like that either. They sued us and asked for a temporary injunction. The judge denied it.

The third lawsuit followed the "Stripping Cartons" spot. This time, they didn't like our taste-test methodology. But we were getting their attention. And we also settled this one to our satisfaction.

• • •

The team should have known that its luck wouldn't hold.

Part of the Fresh'N'Natural story is tied up with the history of Citrus Hill, which was owned by P&G. It jumped right into the premium category with Minute Maid and Tropicana. From the beginning, this was a tough place to be. Because no ingredients were added to not-from-concentrate juice, it was hard for one brand to distinguish itself from another. Citrus Hill was holding onto third place behind the two giants.

In the early 1990s, Citrus Hill attempted to distinguish itself by adding *fresh* to its name—becoming Citrus Hill Fresh Select. A public-interest law firm in Washington, DC, pushed the FDA to get involved. Although it was never proven, Citrus World felt pretty certain that this public-interest firm was paid by one of the big national brands. The FDA ultimately seized thousands of gallons of Fresh Select orange juice from a warehouse in Minneapolis. Although P&G agreed to stop using the term *fresh* on the package, the brand was never able to regain any forward motion.

Citrus World, with its fledgling Fresh'N'Natural brand, should have seen the writing on the wall.

DAVID

Fresh'N'Natural's fourth legal battle came in the spring of 1991, right out of the blue. We were hit by a Mack truck driven by the FDA. I personally think that we were the small guys on the block, but nevertheless, the head of the FDA decided that we could not use the word *fresh* on any product that had been processed, and they singled us out. It didn't matter that the only processing we did was the flash pasteurization. We couldn't use the name. And we couldn't fight the bureaucracy.[1]

WALT

I can remember sitting in Joe Marshburn's office when the call came in from the FDA on a Friday afternoon. I can tell you that I got sick. I knew that if we didn't do something, and do it quickly, we would lose the brand. It would all go down the drain. The FDA magnanimously gave us until Monday morning to tell them the new name.

Unfortunately, all our fallback positions had the word *fresh* in the name. We had no time to do any sophisticated research, so that was out. We were in trouble.

SYL

Boy, that Friday was a day I'll never forget. We had been in the middle of a new image campaign for Fresh'N'Natural when I received the call from Walt about the new FDA ruling and the need to change the brand name. He outlined the government mandates. We had thirty days for new packaging to appear on the shelves, and sixty days for all Fresh'N'Natural to be off the shelves. He also stressed how critical it was that we get high-value coupons in the papers as close to that sixty-day cutoff as possible.

---

1 Susan Spann, *The History of Florida's Natural*, 1995, promotional video.

Well, I assured Walt it would be no problem. When I hung up the phone, I said, "Man, do we have a problem!" I knew that space deadlines for new material had passed two weeks before. The account team's collective shock soon turned into panic. And then we came up with a plan. It would require extraordinary effort from all corners of the agency. And as of yet, there wasn't even a brand name!

WALT

We had to come up with something quick. And we couldn't let panic control us. We used a plan that all the marketing degrees in the world could not have prepared us for.

My strategy was to make up a brand name that wouldn't look significantly different to consumers. So, we needed to replicate the look of the brand logo as closely as possible. John Clarke, Dan McSpadden, Sales Manager Bob Sawatzki, and I gathered in my office. We took out a dictionary. Together, we looked up all the words that started with *F* that might be appropriate for orange juice. We also looked for a word that would somehow work with an apostrophe. With that search, Fresh'N'Natural became Florida's Natural. It seems like a simple idea, but it was far from it.

In those days, there was no Internet trademark research available with the click of a few keys. We used a cumbersome book that listed all trademarked names. And it was only as accurate as its last publication date. After we chose Florida's Natural, we called our lawyer to help. David's son Peter Latham and I divided up any companies whose names we thought might conflict and started calling them. Today, it would be a simple task, but then, it was far from it. Just getting the phone numbers of the brand owners was a chore. After calling, there seemed to be two potential conflicts, but neither one was directly in our category. I rolled the dice and went with my gut, and Florida's Natural was born.

SYL

The good news was that the agency's media team was able to get the ad space secured. But the bad news was the closing date for materials had passed. The newspapers gave us an extension of four days to get the ad ready. By then we had a name, but that was all we had. No packaging, no graphics, nothing. Our team worked through the weekend to come up with the ad. When they put it together, they did it with smoke and mirrors because the ad featured a package that never existed!

• • •

And so, Florida's Natural was born. It was a transformation that basically went unnoticed by consumers, exactly as planned.

KNOX MASSEY, FORMER PRESIDENT AND CEO OF TUCKER WAYNE & COMPANY

Our agency went through some frantic paces during the name and package change. It was a wild time for us all. I wondered how it looked to the outside world—to people who might see the new package and wonder what had happened. One day shortly after all this took place, I was having lunch with the global marketing director of the Coca-Cola Company. Now, of course, Coca-Cola was one of Florida's Natural's biggest competitors. We were talking about our clients, and he brought up Citrus World. He said that the whole name-change episode was the most seamless transformation he'd ever seen in his professional career. I took that as high praise, especially considering the source.[2]

• • •

A more surprising testament to the smooth switch came in a comment from Frank Hunt, board chairman of Citrus World. He tells the story of mentioning to his wife, "I wonder when they are going to put the new name on the package?"

"Honey," she replied, "the new package has been in our refrigerator for the past ten days."

---

2 Susan Spann, *The History of Florida's Natural*, 1995, promotional video.

Fresh'N'Natural morphs into Florida's Natural

WALT

I'll never forget that exhausting weekend. Really one of the worst in my life. But in the end, the brand was actually helped by this process. Florida's Natural turned out to be a much stronger and better name for the brand. We ended up being helped by the very folks who wanted to derail us. When it was all over, we had a higher market share after the name change.

• • •

But that wasn't quite the end of Fresh'N'Natural.

WALT

Our product came through the fire, but what I was left with was a staff that had been singed. For months, we had worked like crazy getting Fresh'N'Natural on the shelves. We promoted it, we sold it, and we restocked it—everyone knew we were throwing everything behind it. Suddenly, it was gone. And the sales team was scared. Sure, we had reacted to the problem with amazing speed and figured out a way to fix things, but there was no guarantee it was going to work. So, I had to come up with something to get the team re-energized.

SYL

What Walt came up with was to stage a mock funeral for Fresh'N'Natural. And I'll tell you, I hope my funeral is as elaborate. We had singing, a eulogy, and a gathering around the "body," which was a carton floated out into the middle of a pool in a child's tube. The entire sales staff, the members of the ad agency, the marketing and manufacturing groups, and even the people from the research-and-development department gathered around to watch as we and the Widow Natural, dressed in a black suit with a full mourning veil over her face, said good-bye to our little friend. Singing a hymn to the tune of "I'll Fly Away," the group finished the ceremony with this verse and chorus:

Verse:
Soon you'll be knocking on St. Peter's gate;
You'll fly away to heaven.
June 6, your final expiration date;
You'll fly away.

Chorus:
You'll fly away, Fresh'N'Natural,
You'll fly away.

FDA says your name just cannot stay,
You'll fly away.

WALT

I remember that Syl delivered the eulogy over Fresh'N'Natural, which probably would have gotten us sued again if anyone from Tropicana had been present. There were lots of references to orange ice and finger-pointing at the big guys who stood to gain from our undoing.

But the capper of the evening was a poem I had asked the agency to write based on A. E. Housman's "To an Athlete Dying Young." (Thanks, Jesuit education!) The real poem opens with a town cheering in honor of a local athlete. The next verse has the same town somberly receiving the body of the deceased athlete, who is being returned to them. The poem goes on to say that the athlete would not have to outlive his fame and would never face the shame of being beaten by another. I wanted Fresh'N'Natural to have that same treatment. I still have a copy of our version of the poem—"To a Brand Dying Young." Here's how it ended:

Now you will not swell the rout
Of brands that wore their honors out.
Juices whom renown outran
And the name died before the brand.

So set, before its sweetness fades,
The taste on which your fame was made.

And hold to lips the new-filled cup
A juice whose name was just made up.

And round that early laureled head
We flock to bury the strengthless dead.
And find that where the old name curls
"Florida's Natural" now unfurls.

And that was the way we buried our brand and introduced the new one. Florida's Natural sat on a stage and was uncovered at the last moment to cheers and laughs. It was even embraced by the Widow Natural. I'd say it was a great way to show our strength and determination.

• • •

The sales, marketing, and advertising team put a great spin on what could have been a calamitous situation. But in reality, this episode marked the end of only a portion of the legal grenades Tropicana lobbed at Citrus World. In an article that appeared in the *Sarasota Herald Tribune* on June 24, 2003, the writer quoted court documents from one of the earliest lawsuits: "'Citrus World's introduction of Fresh'N'Natural pasteurized, ready-to-serve, not-from-concentrate orange juice in April of 1987 marked a landmark challenge to Tropicana's virtual monopoly in the sale of such juice,' Citrus World said in court documents it filed in 1990. 'From the time of Fresh'N'Natural's inception, Tropicana has fought tenaciously to foreclose the product's market entry.'" The writer goes on to say, "What Citrus World officials say they object to most is Tropicana's use of the legal system to maintain its position in the market."[3]

It seems that the big company's marketing staff had strategies up their sleeves too.

---

3 Michael Braga, "Tropicana's Lawsuit Is Dismissed," *Sarasota Herald*, June 24, June 2003, accessed September 12, 2016. http://www.heraldtri-bune.com/news/20030624/tropicanas-lawsuit-is-dismissed

7

The Overhaul

WALT

The lawsuit and name change had been a huge distraction for our company. And even though things worked out to our advantage, these events gave us plenty to think about. We knew it was time to change our strategy. Our first commercial merely announced our presence. The next two targeted Tropicana directly, by name. We had made a grand entrance, but now we needed to stand for something that differentiated us from the big brands. We couldn't just talk about being a premium brand, because there's not much difference between one brand and another. And we couldn't talk about the competition, or they'd sue.

SYL

Walt had charged the agency with creating a brand-positioning campaign for Florida's Natural. He wanted something that would set them apart from the other premium brands. We had many concepts and lots of ideas with kernels of possibility, but nothing was really jumping out at us. Saying our juice tasted better than the other guy's product was not enough to get consumers to choose in our favor.

WALT

I knew the agency was struggling. Selling on taste had been tried and discarded by every juice company, including ours; it simply is not a believable position to consumers. Syl and I had strategy discussions, and we rehashed objectives and strengths, but I wasn't hearing or seeing anything that thrilled me.

Our early attempts at advertising were not brand building. Our ads talked about our competition and not our product. Our advertising budget was pretty small, and we knew we couldn't compete with the big guys with our media buy, so whatever new concept we came up with had to be memorable enough to make an impression in our targeted outlets. We needed something that would be a long-term brand-building idea.

One day, Syl, the agency president, Knox Massey, and the creative team that worked on the account came down to our offices in Lake Wales for a brainstorming session. I gave them a tour of our plant, winding up at the research lab. I explained how our co-op worked, and how we were different from other orange-juice producers, especially our main competitors, who were owned by large soda corporations. We had more than one thousand grower-members who owned more than fifty thousand acres of citrus groves in central Florida. They delivered their fruit to us through thirteen grower associations. This was the way we'd done business since the company started in

1933. The only thing that had changed was the number of grower-members and the end products.

As the group was walking back to the office, Knox just casually said, "Maybe the co-op message is something we can build a brand story around."

This was the first of the agency's big ideas. Out of that casual comment came the line that defined us: "We own the land; we own the trees; we own the company." Suddenly, Florida's Natural had a position and a unique point of difference. We could make a claim that the others couldn't, and it became the basis for our entire brand identity.

• • •

According to Dan McSpadden, the early advertising was tactical, not strategic. "We poked the competition but had to get to a long-term strategy somehow. The co-op message allowed us to move in that direction."

SYL

The agency's creative team ran with that co-op idea. Now, we had a story to tell. And it became a story with many chapters. The early co-op-driven commercials contained three key copy points. Each highlighted different aspects of the grower-owner story and ended with a shot of Florida's Natural juice swirling into a carefully lit glass as the voiceover proclaimed "We own the land; we own the trees; we own the company. And that's a difference you can taste."

Unlike Those Big Juice Companies, Our Idea Of Liquid Assets Is A Little Different.

Florida's Natural® Brand not from concentrate premium juice is made by a co-op of Florida growers whose only business is making juices. They own their land, their trees, their company. Of course, that means they do things a little different from those big juice companies. But, it's a difference you can taste in every glass.

Taste The Difference.

Why does a co-op of Florida growers make such a great-tasting juice?

Because our stockholders meet regularly.

Florida's Natural™ Brand not from concentrate premium juice is made by a co-op of Florida growers whose only business is making juices. They own their land, their trees, their company. Of course, that means they do things a little different from those big juice companies. But it's a difference you can taste in every glass.

Taste the difference.

Finally—an image the brand could build on.

WALT

I remember when the agency came to me with the initial concept, which featured close-ups of growers in the groves carrying crates of oranges. There was a bee on an orange blossom and growers with field ladders. I thought the ideas were great. The creative team proposed using title cards between these scenes, which they promised would be attention-getting and memorable. I think those cards were the trendy thing at the time. But they sold me on them.

SYL

When the spots were being edited, I sat back at the office, waiting for the call to come and approve them. I got to the studio and watched these commercials, which were beautifully shot, with golden lighting, a product that glowed, and the much-hyped title cards. "These are great, guys, but they feel a little long. Has anyone put a clock to them?"

"That's what we need to talk to you about," said the art director. "Can we buy forty-five-second spots instead of thirties?"

Out went the title cards that we had worked so hard to sell to Walt.

WALT

The agency also convinced me that the commercials needed these beautifully etched glasses with our brand logo on them. Well, during the pour shot, the name didn't show up. The art directors loved the look and said it was "subtle and elegant." I hated it. I needed more of the brand name. So, I sent them over to Cracker Barrel to buy a set of plain glasses and stuck some Florida's Natural decals on them. I don't know what it cost me per hour to have the art directors do that, but at least we could read the brand name after the juice was poured.

SYL

We shot in the groves for three days. And we were very proud of our efforts. Although Walt almost drove us crazy in the process.

WALT

When it came time to film the commercials, I'm sure I drove the agency crazy. For one thing, I couldn't stand these big Hollywood-type productions where you had about ten people standing around with only one or two working at any given time. And where union workers hired to do a specific job were not allowed to do anything else. So, it boiled down to too many people getting paid for doing nothing.

SYL

It's awful to be with Walt on a shoot. He has zero patience and no tolerance for spending even an extra dime on something that might enhance the project. Whenever we were working on a commercial, I knew exactly how it would go. We'd set up, usually out in the groves. We'd begin shooting when the light was right; we'd pause to take a break or reset or wipe the Florida sweat off the talent. Inevitably, that's when Walt would show up to see what was going on. He'd look around, make a remark about how nobody was working and how much he was paying for that, and then he'd take off. He always thought we were trying to spend his money by padding the shoot.

WALT

One time, the agency and the hired crew were in the groves to shoot a new television ad. The weather wasn't as cooperative as they would have liked. Well, in Florida, it usually rains a bit every afternoon. Only this time, it was raining in the mornings, wiping out the early morning light. I found out later that the art director had gone to Syl on the third day and said, "We need to move the shoot to California." He talked about the rain as if it were a hurricane. And he was serious! He tried to convince Syl that there was every reason to pick up and head out there.

SYL

I laughed out loud when Mack, our art director, came to me with the suggestion that we reconvene in California. I guess that's why art directors are not account executives. It's hard to support the claim that you own the land and you own the trees if you are not even in your own groves, never mind paying a location fee. I mean, the agency was cutting production costs like crazy—Walt already had the idea to use some of the company's own people in the spots. After all, why not? That's who we were talking about, and that's who we were trying to highlight. Walt would say, "Why hire expensive talent to do what our employees could do?"

Of course, only a few of the employees we used were actual growers, but we pulled a pretty convincing crew together and ended up using some of them for years. There was Raymond, an older guy who was believable and friendly. He entertained us on set with his demonstrations of drinking a glass of orange juice while standing on his head. He had learned the trick drinking beers in a bar.

After Raymond, we transitioned to Jerry, who was younger and perhaps more appealing to our target market.

WALT

Jerry was good-looking and proved so popular that he received several marriage proposals during his time as our star. We got a letter once with a photo that showed a group of college women posing with a cut-out of Jerry that they had appropriated from a grocery store. They had dressed him up in their school colors and written, "I don't know who that Jerry is, but he sure can fill out a pair of jeans." Apparently, the ladies would dress up "Jerry" in the proper attire for the season or the occasion.

SYL

And then there was John Clarke. Good old John Clarke, who ended up causing Walt to pay for a lip-reader. He was in a spot that showed the growers hauling boxes and loading up a truck. There was a scene when they were all taking cool drinks of Florida's Natural after the work was done. They were instructed to laugh and joke with each other—we were using a voiceover, and they would not be heard. But we didn't think being seen would be a problem. In the edit, we kept wondering what John was saying. People were cracking up around him. Finally, we realized that after a long drink, he had put the glass down and said, "That's good shit!" The lip-reader confirmed it, and we had to cover John up a bit before we could use him.

WALT

When you have relatively small budgets that have to compete against big budgets, consistency is key. The great thing about the co-op idea was that it lent itself to so many spin-offs while keeping the core message. We were really the first to use this strategy, and this idea of being responsible for our product from the ground up. So many of our competitors, and other food companies too, use this idea now. And the whole farm-to-table notion has spread everywhere. Other co-ops have nearly copied this positioning. A few years ago, Pepsi's Frito Lay division advertised how they sourced their potatoes![1] So if, as they say, "imitation is the sincerest form of flattery," we have truly been flattered by many companies.

SYL

After the first couple of grower-owner spots ran their courses, Walt charged me with coming up with a new campaign to build on them. We had run the commercials on cable stations and on network television on a limited basis. But they were pretty well worn by the time we started working on replacing them. We knew that we had to continue with the grower-co-op theme, and we didn't want to just tell another story about harvesting our fruit. After our first spot, "Corporate Ladder," we continued to use business terms like "Annual Report," "Stock Growth," "Window Office," and "Family Tree," using visuals of things like new trees, the view from a tractor window, and other things typically found in the groves to make our point.

---

1 Tara Lohan, "Lays Touting Their Potato Chips as Locally Grown—Have They Gone Too Far?" *Alternet*, August 19, 2009, accessed June 30, 2016. http://www.alternet.org/story/142071/lays_touting_their_potato_chips_as_locally_grown_--_have_they_gone_too_far

So, the challenge was twofold: keeping the established co-op brand imagery while keeping the creative product fresh, and taking the brand to the next level. Ultimately, we sought a closer connection with the consumer.

WALT

Over the years, Citrus World's marketing group built a great partnership with the agency's art director, Chuck Mumah, who worked on our account from the time we began our relationship. And although art directors are not supposed to deal directly with clients, I had developed a good personal relationship with Chuck. Over the years, Syl, Chuck, and I had traveled to some exotic places together. I remember one time in the Amazon when group of local natives were so taken with Chuck that we joked that if he stayed a few more days, he would have been made chief.

Anyway, Chuck was part of the creative team working on the new Florida's Natural campaign. One day, and this was typical of Chuck, he faxed me a simple line drawing of a hand in a work glove, handing a Florida's Natural carton to a female consumer. The drawing showed nothing else but the handoff. All the viewer could see of either one of these people were their hands. The image was so simple, but it was iconic and memorable. I was blown away. Here was a symbol that captured our message perfectly. And that's what the best advertising is. We used this handoff idea on everything, all of our collateral, all of our print ads, and all of our TV spots. We even started selling work gloves in the Visitor's Center. It became the image of Florida's Natural.

SYL

The creative team came up with a new tag line: "As close to the grove as you can get." This helped us take a step in a new, but related direction. In our commercials, grocery-store shoppers who were reaching into the chilled juice case for a carton of Florida's Natural actually reached beyond into the daylight as the camera shifted to a grove point of view. The grower would see a hand reach out and, sometimes, with Olympian speed and skill, he would deliver a carton before the hand retreated. Other spots showed grocery-store stockers putting on sunglasses before heading into the back room, which was actually the grove, to retrieve cases of Florida's Natural. We had fun with the spots, and they were well received, and more importantly, fifteen years later, they are still remembered by consumers. Our competitors can't say the same.

• • •

Dan McSpadden confirms their memorability. "I don't know that anybody thought the hand off would end up being the iconic image for the brand. Consumers remember those first spots with the hand coming through the shelf like it was yesterday, and they ran twelve or thirteen years ago. Now I can't imagine a time when the brand won't use this imagery."

WALT

Consistency was also critical to the way our advertising and marketing team was managed. Unlike our competitors, we had the same group in place for the entire time we were developing the brand. For our competitors, their brand managers, ad agencies, and messages changed every few years. At airline companies, when there were problems, the first thing a new president did was repaint the planes. One time, when Delta was having problems, I counted four different color schemes on their planes. In consumer products, when a new VP of marketing is hired, the first thing he or she does is fire the ad agency and introduce a new break-through campaign. In both cases, this approach buys the new manager a few years but rarely does much for the brand. We kept the same brand position and agency the whole time we were building the brand.

8

Partnership

WALT

At Citrus World, the marketing staff was lean, so over time, the agency became our marketing partner. I ran the department and had sales managers over each of our divisions: At Home, Away from Home, International, and Food Service. Our marketing manager was great at looking at reports, analyzing data, and coming up with insights into the marketplace, but mostly, I made decisions based on my intuitions. Unlike other consumer packaged goods companies, Citrus World had only two product managers. Some companies our size had twenty to thirty marketing people. We outsourced many things to the agency. And some of those things really weren't related to advertising. The people at the agency were the experts at creating, buying, and planning media, but we had lots of other things we needed help with.

SYL

Walt would call me up with a crazy idea for a promotion, and it was usually something he needed immediately. Back in the

Donald Duck days, we ran contests, giveaways, special events, whatever. This put us in the business of organizing cruises for prizewinners, designing prizes and incentives, and developing all kinds of promotional materials. All of this should have been handled by a promotions company, but Walt wanted it all to go through the agency.

WALT

Knox had made it clear that he didn't particularly want the agency to be producing collateral material. They made their profits mainly through media placement and the related production. But Citrus World was a small company, relatively speaking, and I knew I could trust Syl to get things accomplished the way I wanted.

• • •

Trust was what Walt was finally starting to feel for the first time in an agency relationship. Syl's calm manner and his attention to detail taught Walt that he could rely on him to pick up the slack. And Syl knew how to bend the rules just enough to be sure Walt got what was needed.

SYL

I went to battle for Walt several times. There was more than one occasion when I trooped into the president's office to justify an expense or project or personnel choice because it would better serve Walt's need and our companies' long-term partnership.

I had an assistant, Sue, who worked with me on the Citrus World account around the time the Florida's Natural brand was just being launched.

Even though Sue retired after her son was born, Walt wanted to keep her involved in his nontraditional agency-directed projects. I was able to keep her on retainer, and we used her for years on special corporate projects. This meant that once each year, I would have to troop into the CFO's office to explain the expense. And each year, after giving him the same reason—"Walt wants her on the account"—her fees were approved.

Sue Spann at work in the 1980s

After a while, agency management stopped arguing with me. Walt was just not going to be a regular client. After I learned to stop walking on eggshells around him, I got to like him even more. He was forceful, blunt, and direct. And he could make a sure and swift decision. With many clients, you have to go through layers and layers of approval to get anything going. Sue always talked about working for one of the agency's biggest business accounts. The comparison between them and Citrus World was startling. The entire time she worked for the other client, they were trying to get a new television campaign approved. It went up through several rounds of managers, each one tweaking or adding a little input. She was pregnant during that time and liked to joke that her unborn child would be starting kindergarten before the commercial ever ran. When she left to have her baby, they were no closer to going into production.

That was never the case with Walt. Everyone on our team knew that the day we made a presentation was the day we would come home with an answer. Sometimes the process was infuriating and discouraging, but sometimes it was invigorating and affirming. Those were the meetings we lived for. You always knew where you stood with Walt. And it was a great feeling to walk away knowing that we had Walt's approval.

Typically, Walt would walk into a meeting empty handed. He would sit down and listen to what we had to say. If we put a document in front of him outlining a media proposal or production costs, he'd skip the first sections and turn directly to the back page to see how much it would cost him. If he liked it, he'd stand up, say okay, and walk out of the room. If he didn't, he'd tell us, "Listen. That's not what we need to do to move the business. Now I don't care how you are going to do this, but here's what needs to be done." Meeting over.

• • •

In a scrapbook compiled to mark Walt's retirement, a few of the sales managers shared similar stories about how Walt conducted meetings. According to National Sales Manager Craig Steensen:

> We would start out with Walt describing the issue, explaining the options and letting the group know how the situation should be handled. Then we would sit around the table discussing the pros and cons of each solution. Maybe a few alternative ideas would be thrown in there, which would begin a new round of dissection. The discussion would go on forever.
>
> By now Walt's patience for the topic would be exhausted. He'd get up and say, "Well, you guys know what I think. I don't want to influence you in any way—handle it how you want. But you know what I think." Meeting adjourned.

Another sales manager, Rick Hernandez, remembers:

> Walt's abrupt approach was not limited to special situations. With Walt, when a discussion was over,

it was over! I witnessed this at the end of my third job interview when John Clarke asked me to have a talk with Walt. Walt stared at me, explained that he had no part in the decision process and if John was okay with hiring me so was he. I was out the door in less than 60 seconds, with a job offer within the hour! I called it a drive-by interview. Later on when I was a manager and brought a prospective employee for Walt to meet I learned that he was equally quick to disqualify someone. A few hours after the brief 60-second interview with Walt, I heard from John Clarke that I needed to keep looking for a suitable candidate."

SYL

After careful prep work, sometimes Walt's quick approval could be as deflating as his shutdown. We would be sitting there, armed with a full staff of media, creative, and account people, who were ready to pitch ideas, justify strategies, or explain the reasoning behind a proposal. It sort of felt like we were all dressed up with no place to go.

WALT

I don't talk much about my time in the army, but there are a few things I learned from my experience there. People like concrete orders; they want to know the mission. It's easy to understand expectations when you are given parameters and know what the objective is.

I know Syl thinks I place a lot of stock in *The Art of War.* But probably more influential to me was a famous essay I read when I first started working. It's called "A Message to Garcia,"[1] and it was first published in a magazine in 1899. This essay has been reprinted hundreds of thousands of times. It tells the story of President McKinley during Cuba's struggle for independence in the Spanish-American War. McKinley wanted to get a message to the leader of the rebel forces there, a general named Garcia. But the problem was no one knew where to find Garcia, who was deep in the mountains of Cuba. McKinley didn't worry about that. He gave his message to a lieutenant, who took it, somehow found Garcia, and delivered the message four days later.

Now the point of that story is that this lieutenant didn't ask where he was supposed to find Garcia, what he looked like, or how to get to him. He just took the message and left.

I've given that essay to every one of my salespeople along the way. I want them to own their jobs. I want them to figure things out and report back when the assignment is completed. Syl is that guy. I could have told him to take a message to Garcia, and he would have left immediately.

• • •

Syl took a lot of messages to Garcia over the years. Some were crazier than others.

---

1 Elbert Hubbard, "A Message To Garcia," *Foundations Magazine*, 1899, accessed June 29, 2016. http://www.foundationsmag.com/garcia.html

SYL

Walt was always coming up with different things for my team to do. He tested us enough times to know that we could get things done for him, so we became his go-to guys for all kinds of projects. But I knew if I made Walt look good, we'd all look good.

And in spite of the tough shell Walt liked to wear around us and the people who worked for him, it wasn't long before we discovered his Achilles' heel—kids. And in particular, his kids.

When Citrus World was still putting money and ads behind Donald Duck, we came up with an idea for an animated commercial that used live actors. And we knew that one way to get the client—any client—to buy into a concept was to draw a storyboard that featured his or her child. We hit the jackpot that time because we were able to use four clients' kids—two of them Walt's, who were about four and six at the time.

The children and their parents showed up on the set in Atlanta, ready for the shoot. As the day wore on and the kids got tired, we were astonished to see a softer side of Walt than we had ever imagined existed. He sat with his kids, held them, spoke patiently to them, and calmed them down. Astonished, Sue and I looked at each other. We were used to walking a straight path with Walt, and we had expected strict treatment to bring the kids back in line. What we witnessed was a velvet touch. Our one-dimensional client, who rarely strayed from the narrow course he laid out for his team, could be derailed. I'd say that was one of the turning points in our understanding of Walt. His shell had a crack!

Every year, Walt would put on a neighborhood Halloween party for his kids. This party became bigger and bigger each year, and soon, he realized he couldn't pull it off by himself. He called me one day and told me what he wanted. Next thing we knew, Chuck Mumah and I were heading down to the Atlanta Farmers' Market to try to purchase fish eyes, pig teeth, and chicken feet to make some sick witches' brew meant to scare all the neighborhood kids. The next year, Walt wanted something else. The thing was—you couldn't say no to Walt.

Sue and I would team up to get some of these crazy things done for Walt. One of his big items each year was the annual meeting. Walt hated the idea of standing up in front of those grower-owners and delivering numbers with a dry slide presentation. He knew they needed to hear that kind of stuff, but he always wanted to give them something more. One year, he had the brainstorm that he would use his salespeople to dance, sing, and deliver props to the stage to illustrate the points he was trying to make. And somehow, he figured that Sue would be the perfect one to pull this together. So, to highlight a new product, which was just entering the West Coast markets, she got a group of sales guys to dress in bathing suits and T-shirts and carry surfboards. They came out dancing to "Surfin' USA," each plunking down a juice bottle on the edge of the stage. To broadcast another product's entry into the New York market, Sue had the sales guys dress in top hats and tails and dance to "New York, New York." I know this was not what she signed up for, but somehow, she pulled it off. I don't think Tropicana and Minute Maid—or Pepsi and Coke—ever entertained their shareholders this way.

Salesmen dancing to the Beach Boys to introduce
a product to the California market

Sue prepping salesman David Jones for a sales meeting
showcase—dancing to "New York, New York"

Bluebird being introduced during the grand finale
of the "New York, New York" number

WALT

These meetings were great. You should have seen my sales guys.
I had spent a lot of time making them professional salespeople
but still made them do stuff like this. All the time.

SYL

Sue and I did other crazy things for Walt, too. One year, he
wanted us to produce a video on Citrus World's new dispenser
system for its away-from-home segment. We were used to
shooting in customer locations—restaurants, institutions, or
grocery stores—but it seemed that this time, the only place

these dispensers were available for us to shoot was in a nudist resort about an hour from Citrus World's offices. So, Sue hired a crew, and we headed up there.

I tell you—this project turned out to be one of those things you never forget. Sue tells the story of her first glimpse of the residents. "As we pulled through the gates, we immediately passed the tennis courts where we saw four people playing mixed doubles. All they had on were tennis shoes and socks. Oh—and maybe there was a visor or two. They were running back and forth, with lots of body parts moving in all directions. All I kept thinking was, 'Doesn't that hurt?'"

My first image was of the back end of a guy bending over to start his lawn mower. Chuck was with Sue and me on that trip, and he captured the moment in a little sketch. I think Sue kept it for years.

We shot the video in the kitchen of the dining hall. While we were setting up, a few couples came in for lunch. They just walked in, sat down on the vinyl chairs, and ordered their meals. I mean they weren't sitting on towels or covered up or anything. The kitchen staff wore hairnets, at least. And most of them were fully dressed. I think Health Department regulations made sure of that. I guess the dining hall doubled as the place for social functions because I noticed a sign on the wall that said No Slow Dancing.

Some of the things our group saw that day we just couldn't unsee. Like the huge woman driving the golf cart. Or the two couples hanging out together by the pool. Sue and I were cracking up wherever we looked. I guess we could be accused of being juvenile and unsophisticated, but one thing I learned that day was that the people who walk around naked in public are the very people you don't want to see naked!

WALT

I had the agency handle lots of special projects for us. For a couple of years, we ran the Florida's Natural Cooking Contest. After sorting through hundreds of entries, we selected our finalists and flew them to Florida. We rented a kitchen trailer with four cooking stations and positioned it in the Grove House Visitor's Center parking area. It was actually a huge production. The setup cost us a fortune. We had four chefs cooking in this glorified trailer. And did I mention this was in Florida? It was springtime, but it was hot in that metal kitchen! They prepped, cooked, and served their dishes to food-industry judges, who included regional chefs and restaurant owners. The winner received a $10,000 cash prize and was featured in a national PR campaign and on our website with the winning recipe.

The cooking contest was another instance where our group learned as we went. None of us knew that there was a circuit of professional contestants. When our finalists showed up, they seemed to know each other. They talked about other contests they had won, and they made lots of demands of our staff. The second time we held this contest, we had a particularly picky competitor. Nothing pleased her. She complained about everything. I'd be lying if I told you it upset me that the dish she was delivering to the judges fell to the ground as she slipped down the ramp leading from the trailer.

SYL

The Citrus World account team got called on to do things no other agency would have done. And truthfully, it made our jobs both more frustrating and more fun. Because we always had budget constraints, we never could do a full-scale production the ideal way, especially when it came to the corporate projects. For instance, every time we worked on a new video, we would ask to schedule the shoot for a time when the groves would look their best. That window is open from November to March. Once it really warms up, the groves are picked clean. But it never seemed to work out for us to shoot during those months since the funds weren't available until late summer. We ended up buying several hundred fake oranges that we could wire into the trees to make a shot look real.

WALT

All of these side projects were always running in the background of the team's main efforts—to build the Florida's Natural brand. Early on—not too long after the launch of the brand—we decided that one way to get more shelf presence was to introduce a new Florida's Natural product. We decided to start with a premium not-from-concentrate grapefruit juice.

Grapefruit was a hard sell. There were only a small number of consumers who drank it, and they did so despite the taste. Canned grapefruit juice was just not appetizing.

We had a surplus of grapefruit in Florida. But Joe Marshburn thought we should use Ruby Red grapefruit from Texas—mostly because of its beautiful red color. I didn't want to do that since Texas fruit is not Florida fruit. Fortunately for me, the year we launched the product, the Texas grapefruit crop was devastated by a freeze. This allowed me to do what I wanted in the first place, which was to use Florida grapefruit. I decided to call our juice Ruby Red anyway. It was a simple thing, but it made all the difference. After our entry, almost every chilled grapefruit juice was called Ruby Red. Consumers didn't want grapefruit juice, but oh, how they liked Ruby Red, even though they were the same. We ran our first batch based on our initial quantity calculations, figuring that we would sell about one-twentieth the amount of the Florida's Natural orange juice we typically sold. But in four months, we sold an entire year's supply! Another innovation for Citrus World—a grapefruit juice that tasted good! This was an easy line extension. And we soon had a number-one market share in the grapefruit category.

Introducing a grapefruit juice that tastes good

Other products followed—Home-Squeezed Style, Growers' Style, Calcium-Added, and then a host of new juice-flavor combinations. All of this helped our brand gain a larger presence on the grocery shelves.

9

Brand Building: Rascals, Rogues, and Renegades

By the end of the 1990s, Citrus World was sharpening its focus on what would become its flagship brand. Just a few years earlier, it had been a co-op without an identity. But a series of calculated steps and a forward-thinking CEO who was willing to back Walt's bold idea changed the course of the company.

WALT

I can't overstate Joe Marshburn's contributions to our growing company. He brought Citrus World through many changes and set us up for the successes we had after he retired. Joe was the ultimate salesman and entrepreneur. And on top of that, he was held in high esteem—inside and outside the company. He has a warm personality and gracious manners. He was the kind of guy who always remembered personal things about other people and made them feel like he cared. He only saw my wife once or twice a year, but each time he did, he asked about the kids—by name. In business, Joe was a risk taker, but his warmth made people feel at ease.

Joe was instrumental in positioning the company to take advantage of the changing marketplace. He was shrewd—and also enjoyed the luck of good timing with some of his more lucrative deals. I count three major endeavors orchestrated by Joe as the reasons we were able to create our Florida's Natural brand.

The first one is that while Joe was CEO, he bought a number of groves at the right time at discounted prices. He then sold them at the peak of the market. Shortly after the sales, most of those groves were devastated in a major freeze.

Next, under his leadership, the company invested in a canning cooperative, which was then sold for far more than its listed value. At the sale, the co-op's partners were to divide up the shares of the business, with the overage to be portioned out in some manner. One of the partners wanted to base distribution of the overage on the number of years each partner had ownership in the company and the number of cans purchased over those years. Well, Joe had other ideas. In the year that Citrus World had ownership in the business, there was a huge spike in purchases of cans due to our shipments during the Gulf War. We were responsible for a 30 percent boost in sales. Joe and the other members of our negotiating team, Steve Caruso and Bob Turner, wanted to base the share calculations on that year's sales alone. This would increase our share of the proceeds by millions of dollars and correspondingly lower the other owners' proceeds by an equal amount. Furthermore, Joe said that if the co-op didn't want to do it that way, Citrus World wouldn't sell. The others reluctantly agreed. We made a ton of money on that deal. Twenty years later, I met the guy who wanted the overage based on historical purchases; he had not forgotten the episode. I think his exact words were "whatever happened to that SOB? I think his name was Marshburn."

And most importantly, Joe started the grove-development projects in South Florida. He sparked the purchases of three pieces of land that were divided into smaller blocks and sold to our members. The growers benefitted from the efficiencies of large grove maintenance and production, but their investments were much smaller. All of the fruit produced in those groves went into our juice. This guaranteed high quality and protection from the freezes that were more frequently hitting the Central Florida groves.

The point of all this is that under Joe's leadership, Citrus World was able to raise enough capital to reengineer our factory and have high-quality fruit to produce Florida's Natural.

And Joe's enthusiasm for the creation of the Florida's Natural brand helped get it launched.

• • •

The late 1980s saw other fortuitous changes at Citrus World.

In 1986, the cooperative bought the family-owned Southern Fruit Company, which was based in Orlando. Their main product was Bluebird juice. This acquisition proved to be a bridge to major new business and opened up additional distribution channels. Bluebird brought in new accounts and, most importantly, a book of international business.

With the acquisition of Bluebird came Steve Caruso, grandson of the Southern Fruit Company founder. Caruso would become Citrus World's next CEO.

WALT

When Steve came on board, he was the perfect second act to Joe Marshburn. Steve was a lot more reserved than Joe, but he cared deeply about people. He changed Citrus World's culture and demonstrated a genuine respect for his employees. He challenged people to take responsibility for their jobs. He was rarely involved in sales and marketing except to show support for the marketing team's plans. In twenty years, Steve did not change any significant item in the annual sales and marketing plan. Steve was an accounts or finance guy at heart. He was also detailed and focused on the company. He worked to build an organization to support the brand.

While Steve was CEO, he led the company through the turbulent times of hurricanes, oversupplies, and freezes. We had some rough stretches, but he kept us steady.

• • •

One of Steve's major accomplishments was the marketing agreement he implemented with the growers. It held members to a committed quantity of fruit to be delivered each year. In the past, the cooperative would accept whatever amount the growers delivered, which led to an unpredictable juice supply. With this new agreement, the company was guaranteed a consistent supply of fruit.

WALT

It was not long after Steve became CEO that Florida's Natural reached a major milestone—national distribution. This was huge for many reasons, not only because of the status obtained by having a national brand but also because it represented a determined effort on our part to capture the country market by market. Most major brands take eighteen months after market tests to roll out across the country. And each new product launch costs about a minimum of $35 million. Between advertising, slotting allowances, broker fees—it costs a fortune. That's why it took Florida's Natural seven years, from 1987 to 1994! We used existing markets to fund the next one. Early on, our growers subsidized the brand's launch by taking lower returns for their fruit. They had a vision, and we had a strategy. By 1994, our last market—Denver—finally clicked into place. It was a day of celebration.

• • •

Director of Marketing Dan McSpadden notes, "A big company would have rolled out all at once and been first everywhere, but we were always hemmed in by budgets so we couldn't do that. Still, we had some victories along the way. We introduced out west before Tropicana and they immediately followed on our heels. From then on it was a footrace to be the first to get to national distribution. Looking back, I think we managed the race just right."

SYL

The agency's media team had been able to buy spots for Citrus World on regional network TV during Florida's Natural's seven-year rollout period. We filled in the gaps of distribution along the way with Donald Duck ads where necessary. This strategy gave us more buying power and allowed us more efficiency.

Once we hit national distribution, we were able to buy national TV ads on morning shows like ABC's *Good Morning, America* and NBC's *Today Show*. We were even able to use our new buying clout to get *Today* weatherman Willard Scott to record a special message to our owners for the annual meeting.

Budget restraints pitted against double-digit network-rate increases kept us from expanding our ads into other even more expensive day parts, particularly prime time. And with the major competitive brands dominating all network TV day parts, we were soon forced into trying a new strategy. We decided to shift Florida's Natural's TV dollars into the growing segment of cable TV. There, the competition was hard to even find.

At that time, cable's total consumer reach was lower than the networks', but it provided a large enough base for us to build a consistent brand message. Just as importantly, it allowed us to provide a stronger level of brand exposure to consumers over a much longer period of time and at a *much* more affordable cost.

Soon, Florida's Natural was running in spots on more than twenty cable television networks for twenty-nine weeks. There were lots of perks and product features that came with that.

One time, Florida's Natural was invited to send someone to appear in a segment on a morning cable show. We decided to feature Mandy Hancock, one of our brand managers. Mandy was smart and beautiful. In fact, as a former Florida citrus queen, she was a perfect representative for the brand.

Mandy and Sue flew to New York to tape the show, where Mandy was to make a citrus smoothie on camera. The test run went perfectly. Then hosts cued the live segment. There was lots of chatter about the product and the delicious things you could make with it. Mandy loaded the blender with fruit and juice, and when the conversation stopped, she pressed the button. With a big smile, she turned off the blender and lifted it up to pour. Well, the blender's bowl had never been screwed back into the base after the test run and came off alone. Smoothie ran out everywhere. But Mandy showed her beauty-queen skills and simply smiled and moved on. We were obviously still working on our prime-time act.

WALT

Even though the brand now had national distribution, we still had to fight for shelf space. Lots of times, the big guys would introduce a new product just to push a smaller player off the shelf. This happened to us several times. Shelf space is the most valuable thing in a grocery store—and the most limited. The major brands would play on category managers' weakness—making numbers for the quarter. The brands might offer inducements (i.e., cash) if the buyers would remove us. Then the brands would put in line extensions and essentially buy us off of the shelves.

We had two major events that really rocked us during those years. And they both ended up helping us in the long run. But at the time, we didn't see it that way.

One morning, I woke up to find out that we had lost brokers in fifteen markets. This was huge! And something we never expected.

Two major companies, Clorox and Coca Cola, had forced a roll-up of brokers, which meant that several brokers were merging together. Their new, shared client list would create conflicts of interest. We were told that because the new larger firms would represent our larger competitors, Florida's Natural would be dropped. This happened in both East Coast and West Coast markets. We were scrambling.

My sales and marketing staff took a long hard look at the way we operated and made a pledge never to use any national firms again. We hired all small brokers who were involved in their individual markets. Our broker relationships became much stronger as a result.

Another disaster was when we got dropped from about 1,200 stores of a major chain. We had been pushed out of some other regional chains before, but suddenly we were out of 1,200 stores. The chain worked on a category management system.

Coke had introduced a new product—Simply Orange—and the chain needed to find space for it. They decided we didn't have enough customer loyalty, so we could be ousted. We were delisted in 2003, and it took us seven years to get back in. But then two things happened. The first was that our consumers started a campaign to get us back into the store. They wrote letters, they talked to store managers, and they bought our product elsewhere. The chain had figured it wouldn't lose sales, that people would just buy another brand.

This led the marketing team to another fortuitous decision. We had been selling to the stores without focusing on building loyalty. We had been cutting deals with the grocery managers and running coupons and specials. The consumer response to our absence from their grocery stores told us that we needed to focus on brand loyalty instead. This was a wake-up call. And building brand loyalty became our number-one priority.

SYL

From then on we hammered the building-brand-loyalty theme everywhere we could, including at sales meetings, on T-shirts, on handouts, and in presentations. Our grower co-op message was well-established by then, so we had a story to tell. We sharpened our message.

Our brand began to reinforce its identity. We started with targeted direct mail, but the cost to reach our audience grew prohibitive. Soon, we shifted to using a loyalty-building tactic that could deliver the numbers we needed at a lower and much more effective cost. A series of three customized eight-page inserts appeared in targeted national magazines. These inserts highlighted the brand's co-op story and included coupons, recipes, and gardening and travel tips. This was really the springboard for future efforts in consumer promotions, digital campaigns, and social media advertising. In fact, Florida's Natural was the first major orange-juice brand to reach over one million friends on Facebook!

Once consumers became invested, it was easier to put our brand in their refrigerators.

WALT

Around this time, the tone of the company's annual meetings began to change. I always tried to be the entertaining part of the program because I could think of nothing more deadly than standing up in front of our growers and spouting out a list of market facts, especially when we really had little to report. Those were the days of the dancing salespeople and humorous videos. Eventually, though, our story developed, and we had something interesting to talk about. I still tried to deliver the news with a bit of a twist, but our strong sales numbers and new products and increased market share let me take a back seat to the progress we were making. I received a nice compliment from Frank M. Hunt II, our longtime chairman of the board. In an article about my retirement, he was quoted as saying, "People looked forward to Walt's reports most at annual meetings, so he often got to speak last and wrap up the meeting."[1]

---

1 Tacey Callies, "Building a Brand," *Citrus Industry*, December 2012.

Frank M. Hunt was really a guiding light during the creation of the Florida's Natural brand. In the early years, when the company was first trying to get the brand going, there was no monetary benefit we could sell to our grower-members. In fact, it didn't make financial sense at all. But Frank had the foresight and vision to convince the grower-members to go along with the plan. When they voted to approve our new product, it was because of Frank's leadership.

Years after the brand was solidly established, I spoke to Citrus World's CPA, who told me that early on, when he was doing the company returns and we were losing so much money, he wondered why we didn't drop this brand. He wanted to end the rollout early. I hope he was glad to see how it turned around!

10

A Little Help from Our Friends

WALT

Looking back at the way the brand grew and developed, it's interesting to see how many times Florida's Natural's competitors helped us out. I am sure they had no idea of the unintended consequences of their aggressive tactics.

Tropicana and Minute Maid are giants. They think like giants, act like giants, and to our advantage, move like giants. When you are a small company on a limited budget, you have to be nimble and flexible and able to react quickly to a situation. These two corporate brands have multiple layers between the product and the top decision-makers. It's different at Citrus World—we always knew all of our growers by name. And many days, we ate lunch with the folks on the production line. So, if there was something going on with the package or the product, we knew right away.

Because of their cultures, large companies are forced to try to innovate. All their marketing employees have to justify their existences. So, they come up with new products or new processes. Florida's Natural's two major beverage competitors introduced a steady stream of new juice ideas. Almost without exception, these were hugely expensive failures. I think Tropicana tried juice with fiber three or four times.

I had a chart that showed Tropicana's innovations over a ten-year period. Often, when they introduced a new item, at a cost of at least $35 million, their market share declined. And one after another, most of those new products ultimately failed. One time, Tropicana even tried a loyalty program that awarded points and prizes for buying cartons. I joked at the time that it wouldn't be long before they brought back S&H Green Stamps.

Their temporary gains in shelf space were offset by the fact that there were no incremental sales increases or profits. More products divided up the same shrinking pie while they were spending additional money on advertising, slotting, packaging, and so on. To our benefit, all of this activity distracted them from orange juice, their main product.

The retailers didn't like all of the new stock-keeping-units (SKUs), but they were happy to take the slotting money and promotional dollars. The new items built inefficiencies into the system and didn't increase the juice category.

And the consumers found it all confusing. For example, in looking for calcium, they might grab the juice with added fiber. Or when they wanted pulp, they might grab a different flavor. By necessity, the Florida's Natural lines were much more straightforward.

Aside from a host of rotating products, it seemed as if Tropicana had a revolving door of brand managers as well. I imagine that being assigned to work on the Tropicana line as its market share declined from 70 percent to less than 30 percent was hardly a plum assignment.

$$\bullet \quad \bullet \quad \bullet$$

As a lean operation, Citrus World gave each sales manager the authority to make decisions about their sales within their budget parameters. This was not always true of the way others ran their businesses.

WALT

At some point, the competition put a new management layer between its sales people and its customers in the form of a financial analyst who would look at the numbers before a promotion to determine the results that promotion would yield to the company and to the customer. Maybe this was a brilliant idea, but all I know is it slowed down the process. I always wanted my sales team members to get to know the customer. They could go on a sales call and quickly decide whether a deal made sense. They didn't have to run it through several people to get an okay. Plus, the competitor's salespeople soon became rolled into a conglomerate of three brands, and they rotated frequently from brand to brand. The salespeople didn't have the chance to make relationships. In our company, we would get a call from a customer offering an open slot for some of our product and could tell them immediately whether it worked for us. We weren't waiting for an analyst to say yes or no.

It wasn't just the number-one brand that moved slowly. One time, we had a very large customer who was filing for bankruptcy reorganization. They were scheduled to run a competitor's ad and needed product. The bankruptcy announcement stalled the process for that competitor, who told the customer it wouldn't ship the product for the ad. I know the reason was because the decision had to be sent up the ladder for approval. Meanwhile, the category manager at the chain called me and said he needed juice, and I sent him the product. And Florida's Natural has reaped the benefits of that quick decision for ten years. Every time we had a business review, the category manager made a point to replay the story for their current CEO.

I had worked at a big company in my early years, but I got another glimpse into how those corporations worked when I attended a marketing conference. One of the featured presenters was a VP from Coke who spoke on the theme of empowering employees. I thought, "Well, this is going to be good. She's a Coke VP—I'm sure she knows what she is talking about."

As it turned out, her job was to be VP of collateral materials. Basically, she was a VP tasked to buy signs.

She proceeded to launch into this long presentation and told a story about how her team had some signs printed up for a promotion. And there was a problem with them—they were the wrong color red. "So, I told my employees to just get it fixed!" she said triumphantly. Surely she had bigger things than that to let her employees handle.

In the late 1980s, our team sat back and watched as Minute Maid went through some problems of its own making. For

years, their black-carton orange juice was the number-one premium from-concentrate juice on the market. The growth of
Tropicana and Florida's Natural convinced them to launch
Minute Maid Premium Choice. The problem was even though
Premium Choice was a good product in an innovative package,
they couldn't bring themselves to say it was better than the black
carton.

Billed as "The gourmet orange juice," this premium version was Minute Maid's top-of-the-line product. But they
were already claiming that their black-carton from-concentrate
juice was as good as any not-from-concentrate juice. It was
positioned to compete with Tropicana and Florida's Natural.

There were ads for Minute Maid Premium Choice that
showed it appealing to bluebloods everywhere. Another ad
showed it on the Trump shuttle, an iconic image of early 1990s
wealth and privilege.

Confusion abounded. Premium Choice was ultimately
abandoned. Minute Maid finally had to introduce a new premium product, Simply Orange, to get away from using its own
name in competition with its black-carton from-concentrate
product. Simply Orange had an eye-catching, unique package
that really set it apart from the others in its category. First of
all, it was only fifty-eight ounces, six ounces less than most
others. It was priced higher than other not-from-concentrate
brands and soon took over the premium spot among orange
juices. This was another gift to us. Traditionally, we had to sell
our sixty-four ounce product for ten cents less than Tropicana's
to make our market share. When Simply Orange came out,

Tropicana wasn't the top premium anymore, and we didn't have to sell our juice for a lower price than Tropicana's.

Simply Orange was a big success. It was regular not-from-concentrate orange juice in a beautiful package. Minute Maid charged more for it, and people bought it. Traditionally, when a new product entered a category, the second and third brands were the ones that suffered market-share loss. In this case, the entire market share that Simply Orange achieved came from the market leader, Tropicana. And at the same time, Florida's Natural's market share grew by 30 percent.

One of the biggest, most expensive blunders Tropicana ever made came in 2009 when they hired the design guru Peter Arnell to give them an updated look. Arnell had just come off of a "breathtaking" (as Arnell himself called it) but highly criticized redesign of the Pepsi logo.[1] As a company that operates in over two hundred countries, you can imagine how many packages, trucks, and signs had to be redesigned and replaced. It is mind-boggling to think of how expensive that move was.

Arnell was correct in that the redesign would increase market share, but it happened for Florida's Natural!

He reimagined the Tropicana carton, removing the iconic straw-in-an-orange image and replacing it with a generic-looking glass that made the carton look as if it were a private-label brand.

----

1 Jim Edwards, "Pepsi's Nonsensical Logo Redesign Document: $1 Million for This?" *CBS News*, February 10, 2009, accessed June 30, 2016. http://www.cbsnews.com/news/pepsis-nonsensical-logo-redesign-document-1-million-for-this/

This package lasted about six weeks. Consumers hated it. The old carton soon made it back to the shelves, and the only carryover from the expensive new redesign was the new orange twist cap. Florida's Natural could never have done something like that and survived.

This adventure is still being told as a cautionary tale. In *Business Insider* magazine, it was used as an example of how new design can go horribly wrong. The article is titled "This Logo Change Caused Tropicana Sales to Plunge."

"About five years ago [Tropicana] went to this very clean but kind of cold-looking logo, and **their sales dropped 20 percent in one month.** Some pundits said they weren't recognizable," [marketing veteran Dennis] Ryan said. "Tropicana has something like eight feet in the refrigerated section. People recognized it. They didn't trust [the new logo]."

People don't like change. And when a logo or packaging for a favorite product changes, it creates trust issues. The package has changed and they wonder if what's inside has, too. The generic logo made people expect a generic product.[2]

2 Max Nisen, "This Logo Change Caused Tropicana Sales to Plunge," *Business Insider*, September 2013, accessed June 30, 2016. http://www.businessinsider.com/tropicana-packaging-change-failure-2013-9

I remember finding out about Tropicana's new packaging. John Clarke was at a meeting when it was introduced to the market. He immediately called me and said, "Walt, I've seen the new package. It's terrible. Get ready to sell a bunch of juice!"

• • •

With the grower-co-op theme, Florida's Natural had firmly established its brand identity. Many generations of ads and marketing strategies descended from the first bold idea of connecting the company to its growers. Florida's Natural had become a brand consumers could trust.

In 2009, Florida's Natural fell into an opportunity to bring the brand to the next level. And this opportunity was another presented by their main competitor—Tropicana.

For much of Tropicana's long history, it had conducted business as a stand-alone company. Over time, it was sold, first to Beatrice and then to Seagram's. It still operated independently, making autonomous decisions.

But then, it was purchased by PepsiCo. At first, it existed as a subsidiary of the giant corporation, but then later, as a cost move, it became a division of PepsiCo. And that's when the game changed.[3]

3 Constance L. Hays, "PepsiCo to Pay $3.3 Billion for Tropicana," *New York Times*, July 21, 1998, accessed June 30, 2016. http://www.nytimes.com/1998/07/21/business/pepsico-to-pay-3.3-billion-for-tropicana.html?module=Search&mabReward=relbias%3Ar; David Salamie and "Tropicana Products, Inc.," International Directory of Company Histories, 1999, "Tropicana

WALT

As a division of PepsiCo, Tropicana was no longer in a situation to make its own decisions, which became increasingly focused on goals and projections and not on the citrus industry. Tropicana decided that it could go outside of Florida—outside of the United States in fact—to find a cheaper source of off-season juice. And as a bonus, the added supply of imported not-from-concentrate juice could be leveraged to keep the cost of fruit from Florida growers lower. Tropicana's people figured it wouldn't matter to consumers where they got their fruit, reasoning that consumers don't care about the origin of juice—just the taste.

At that point, I seized the opportunity to turn Tropicana's decision into something positive for Florida's Natural. As soon as I heard of Tropicana's plan, I decided we would direct all of our efforts to an All-Florida platform.

SYL

Walt's initial directive was to create carton stickers, cap hangers, and point-of-purchase materials declaring that Florida's Natural juice was 100 percent made from Florida oranges. What started out as a tactical plan morphed into a full-blown idea and the beginning of a major strategic shift in creative campaigns for the brand.

Products, Inc.," *Encyclopedia.com*, HighBeam Research, 2006, accessed June 30, 2016, International Directory of Company Histories. http://www.encyclopedia.com/social-sciences-and-law/economics-business-and-labor/businesses-and-occupations/tropicana-products

In addition to Walt's request, we also produced a customized TV spot, built a web page dedicated to the All-Florida theme, offered online promotions and games and invited consumers to play "Take the Test," a guessing game that dominated our website. We showed packages of Simply Orange, Florida's Natural, and Tropicana and asked, "Where does your juice come from?" Consumers would pick one of the three brands, which would reveal the source of the juice, printed right on each package. This clearly showed the competitors using juice from Florida and Brazil and only Florida's Natural's juice being solely from Florida.[4]

• • •

With the All-Florida story resonating so well with consumers, Walt pushed for something more aggressive.

SYL

The agency then created the I Believe campaign. New thirty-second TV commercials featured company spokesperson Dave Crumbly standing in a grove on top of an orange crate proclaiming facts about things he believed in. And of course, the ad included his thoughts about orange juice and where it should come from. Online promotions and games were developed,

---

4 "Where Does Your Orange Juice Come From?" *Literary Food Studies*, September 10, 2015, accessed June 30, 2016. https://literaryfoodstudies. com/2015/09/10/where-does-your-orange-juice-come-from/

along with two customized interactive webpages. The first showed a virtual orange grove where consumers could pin an orange on a statement they believed in. Consumers could also create an avatar of themselves standing on top of an orange crate, broadcasting their closely held beliefs.

Florida's Natural's legal history taught us that we had to be careful in how we represented our competition. Believe me, we had much internal discussion about avoiding lawsuits. Eventually though, we came to realize that maybe a lawsuit would not be the worst thing because of all the attention we could gain. That was when Walt decided we needed to pull the stops and develop a full-blown competitor-directed campaign. It was decided that if our competitors were stupid enough to sue us, it would be the best publicity we could get.

Our most aggressive move was a comparison ad that showed a Tropicana carton and a Florida's Natural carton side by side with magnified blocks of copy that answered the question, where does your orange juice come from? Tropicana's carton said, "Contains orange juice from the United States and Brazil." The Florida's Natural carton said, "100 percent Florida."

The side panels of the Florida's Natural carton showed photos of some of our growers. The headline read, "We can tell you where our orange juice comes from. In fact, we can tell you who it comes from."

A new series of print ads and digital material followed the carton and also hit the All-Florida message pretty hard. Florida's Natural stayed with this campaign for three years.

It Almost Seems Simple

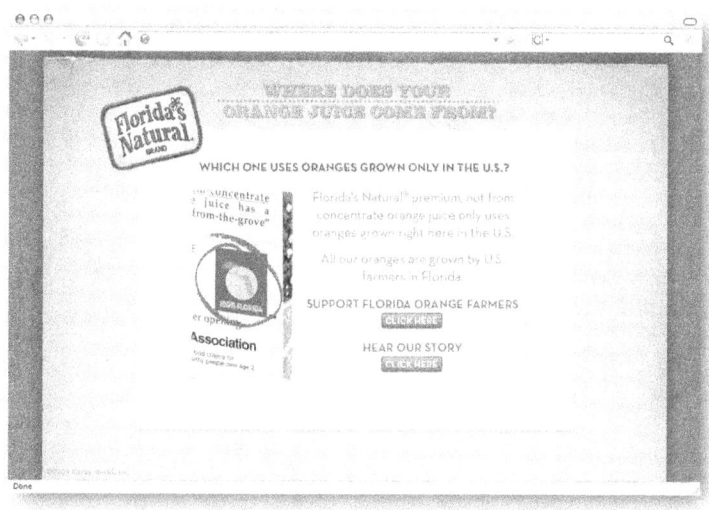

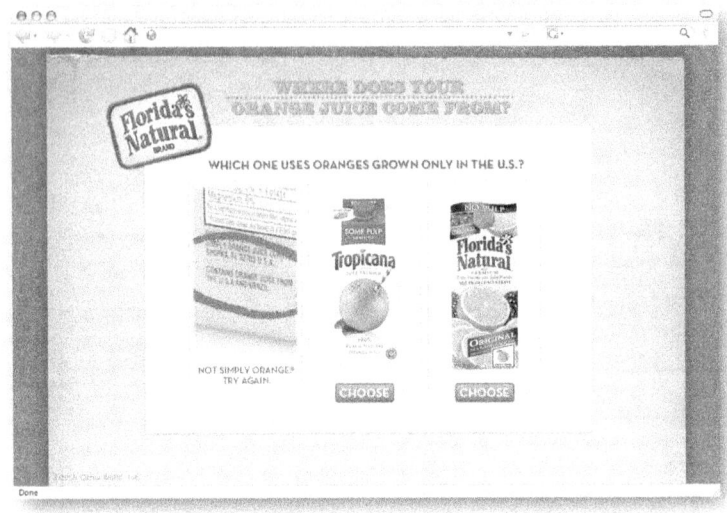

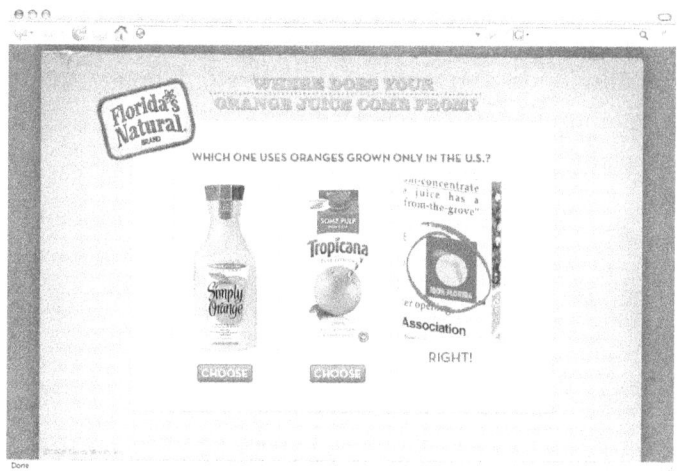

The first "All-Florida" digital campaign

Syl working on the Florida's Natural brand

WALT

The All-Florida campaign produced record results for the brand, and we think it made Tropicana reconsider. It wasn't long before it reintroduced Florida as the source of its own juice.[5]

---

5 "Tropicana Goes Back to Using Only Florida Oranges," *Chicago Tribune*, January 16, 2012, accessed June 30, 2016. http://articles.chicagotribune.com/2012-01-16/business/chi-tropicana-goes-back-to-using-only-florida-oranges-20120116_1_carbendazim-minute-maid-orange-juice-florida-crop; Caroline Scott-Thomas, "Tropicana's Pure Premium Returns to Florida Oranges," *FoodNavigator-USA.com*, January 19, 2012, accessed June 30, 2016. http://www.foodnavigator-usa.com/Markets/Tropicana-s-Pure-Premium-returns-to-Florida-oranges

11

Global Issues

I n 1986, Citrus World acquired the business of the Southern
Fruit Company. The two main assets were the Bluebird brand
of canned juices and Steve Caruso.

The Bluebird family of juices provided an opening to
global markets for Citrus World, especially in the Middle
East, Canada, and the Caribbean. As those markets and consumers matured, Florida's Natural was eventually integrated
into the company's mix of export products. A dedicated
sales-and-marketing team handled the international business,
often learning, and sometimes stumbling, along the way.

WALT

When the export team and I made our first overseas trips,
we had to learn to go along with whatever the prevailing culture dictated. This made for some interesting experiences.
Naturally, food plays an important part in any culture, so over
the years, I learned to eat whatever our hosts served—whether
it was the darkest, strongest coffee in Saudi Arabia or part of a

lamb's unmentionables in Lebanon. Sushi is now a mainstream food in the United States, but thirty years ago, it was exotic. I think the Japanese appreciated that I would eat whatever they offered. In many markets, ethnic Indians are dominant in the food-supply chain. Growing up in Arizona, I learned to eat spicy foods, which was a real asset when eating curry with Indian customers. In Asia, where ethnic Chinese people dominate the markets, I would eat whatever was served. In many cases, I ate parts of animals or fish that would turn an average American green. On more than a few occasions, customers and partners would say, "Walt, you are the only American we have ever seen that can eat like a local." Sometimes, my boss would travel with me. We might be having lunch at a very high-end Chinese restaurant, but if he could, he would order a club sandwich.

I made my first visit to China in 1982. The group I was with took me out for Peking duck at the same restaurant where Chou En-Lai hosted Richard Nixon. I'm not sure why, but somehow it was determined that I was the senior person, and I was served the duck's feet with the solemnity of a ritual. I chewed them and smiled. My colleagues asked, "How were they?"

"Well, about equivalent to eating a small shoe," I told them.

• • •

With the purchase of Bluebird in 1986, Citrus World inherited an export business centered on selling steel cans to the Middle East and Caribbean Islands.

The steel can was the original single-strength package in the US orange-juice market, and it was used in Florida's processed-juice market as early as the 1930s. The can was a perfect package for the early US markets because it didn't need refrigeration; in fact, the can itself was a preservative. The tin salts in the cans' walls kept the juice from browning. The obvious drawback of the package was since it was hot packed, or cooked, it left the juice with a cooked flavor.

In the developed markets, the introduction of Tetra Pak supplanted steel cans as the primary source for at-home consumption of citrus juices. Tetra Pak was not an ideal package for citrus flavors, but it had the advantage of being cheaper. And it could be produced locally. By the 1990s, canned juices in the United States were limited to grapefruit juice and a few other varieties for food-service applications. However, in the world's developing markets, the can was still an appealing package.

WALT

Anyone visiting Dubai today can hardly imagine that in 1986, Bluebird cans were the premium brand. No big Indian wedding or major party would dare serve any juice but Bluebird for fear of disappointing the guests. In Saudi Arabia, thousands of little distributors working out of spaces the size of garages sold Bluebird cans to the nomads and citizens from small villages. One of the brand's key assets for the Saudi shopkeepers was that rats couldn't eat through the metal. In 1986, Citrus World shipped several hundred thousand cases of cans to the Middle East.

The inherited Bluebird business gave our company insight into the values and challenges of exporting. We started doing business with dozens of small distributors. These distributors by and large shared a number of traits that made them successful. They were born entrepreneurs. They were risk takers and in most cases had started with almost no money. They also had a strong belief that truth was not absolute but rather fungible. An old joke was, how do you tell if a distributor is lying? His lips are moving.

A distributor in a developing market takes ownership of a product and resells it to the retailers and wholesalers in his markets. Credit is the lifeblood of the business in a developing market. Retailers are slow to pay the distributors, and the distributors are slow to pay the suppliers. The first and most important rule our group learned in exporting was to get the money. Of course, until you're paid for a product, you're dealing in philanthropy.

Payment can come in many forms, such as cash, letters of credit, or bank guarantees. Over the years, our salespeople weeded out the slow-pay problems, but in the early years, we were more like a collection agency than a sales force. Every time we thought we had a foolproof payment system, one of those clever distributors would find a way to delay payment or stiff us. In my last years, we had zero bad debts in export; it was so unusual the auditors double-checked it.

After the partition of India, millions of Sindhi Hindus left Pakistan for India. Sindhis are amazing business people. I believe as the old adage goes, "If you put a Sindhi in Nome, Alaska, he would sell snow cones at a profit."

Over the years, our group met many Sindhi who were fine moral and ethical business people. But then, there were the others.

In Dubai, our largest Bluebird distributor was a Sindhi. The story goes that he got his start as a distributor by basically grabbing his father-in-law's business. He worked in a bank at the time and read all of the bank customers' letters of credit and his father-in-law's letters of credit. In his spare time, this distributor started importing products and undercutting his father-in-law's prices since he knew them from the letters of credit. Soon, his father-in-law was out of business.

The distributor attended the world's largest food show in Cologne, Germany, which is called ANUGA Food Fair. In order to feel safe, he brought all his salesmen with him so none of them could do what he had done to his father-in-law in the early years. He rented one room in Bonn, and he slept in the bed, and his eight salesmen slept on the floor.

The distributor was supposed to deal in Bluebird products only for catering and food service, but of course, he couldn't resist selling to retail outlets. But retail in Dubai was handled by another distributor. The first distributor would undercut the retail distributor's price. When we confronted him, he jumped up in a very agitated manner declaring, "On my children, I have never done it!" He knew we knew he was lying. I think unless he was ripping someone off, he didn't feel good. Today, we don't do any business with him, but he is extremely wealthy.

The distributor's counterparts in retail ran grocery stores in the United Arab Emirates and Africa. They distributed our products to their stores and others. They too were Sindhis. They were honest and ethical. A huge part of their income went to charity, including a major hospital in the United Kingdom. Today, they don't sell Bluebird but do sell Florida's Natural in their United Arab Emirate stores.

• • •

Having international distribution channels gave Walt a new goal: making Florida's Natural a global brand. He and his sales team traveled from market to market. Most American food brands had local offices and local personnel. So, when the top marketing officer of an American brand showed up from the United States, it was something different. The customers felt a closer connection to the brand because they had a direct relationship with the key people.

WALT

Today, Florida's Natural sells in nearly sixty countries. Of course, like the brand itself, this started in a small way and has grown year after year.

One of our first international opportunities was to sell one-liter cartons of Florida's Natural in Canada. We revised the carton artwork and set to work on the translations. We figured that a direct conversion of our tag line, selling points, and side panels would do the trick, and we hired a translator to help us. We had sold Donald Duck chilled juice in France for many years. "How hard could it be to make a Canadian carton?" we thought.

Well, this translator was not acquainted with the vagaries of French in Quebec. In any language, words can have different meanings. In a direct translation of our copy from the US label, which boasted No Preservatives, the translator inserted the line, "Pas de préservatif." The unfortunate thing was that in Quebecois French, we were declaring that there were no condoms in the package. We quickly found a new translator.

As Florida's Natural entered other markets, we learned a lot about varying cultures and were sometimes shocked by our cultural differences. Japan gave our team a real education.

In the late 1980s, under pressure from the US government, Japan finally allowed the importation of citrus juices.

These were boom times in that country. At one point, it was said that the real estate value of just Tokyo was greater than that of all the real estate in the United States.[1] Japanese companies had a touch of arrogance and superiority.

We negotiated with the Kirin Company for a whole year to introduce Florida's Natural into Japan. At the very last minute, the chairman of Seagram's, which owned Tropicana, made a deal with the Kirin chairman for Kirin to sell Tropicana. It was understandable since Seagram's had business relationships with Kirin, but it meant that we were out.

Our fallback was to go with Suntory. Suntory was an old-line whiskey and beverage company controlled by the

---

1 Michael Browning, "Japan's Land Boom Spilling Across the Sea," *Chicago Tribune.* November, 1989, accessed March 22, 2017. http://articles.chicagotribune.com/1989-11-19/business/8903110641_1_landprices-national-land-agency-rockefeller-center

Torii family. Although we never did a deal to launch Florida's Natural with Suntory, it led to one of the most memorable business meetings I ever participated in.

Steve Caruso and I were to meet Shin Torii, son of the founder of Suntory. We went to the top floor of the Suntory building. The floor was more like a high-rise palace than a place of business. Mr. Torii's male assistant ushered us into the throne room, also known as Mr. Torii's office. Chairman Torii sat on a platform two feet above the floor that overlooked the biggest office I'd ever seen.

After the assistant introduced us to the emperor of Suntory, rather than turning and walking out, he bowed and backed out in a bent-over sign of submission or respect, without making any eye contact. The emperor-chairman came down. We sat with a translator. When Steve and I conducted international business meetings, I usually handled the business discussion after the introduction and formalities. In this case, since I was not the senior person, when I would speak, the translator would translate, and the chairman would address Steve. Since only I knew the particulars of our discussion, we continued on in this bizarre fashion to the conclusion of the meeting.

The Japanese are sticklers for perfect packages. A drop of glue or a scratched label is not acceptable. Whenever we started filling a new package, the Japanese would send over a delegation of inspectors who would monitor every point on the production line, looking for miniscule defects. On one run, our VP of operations, Charles Matthews, came to me and said, "This is crazy." He pointed out that no one was checking the taste of the juice—all the inspectors were doing was driving him crazy examining the packages. Unlike in America, where people worried about what was inside the package, in Japan, people were fixated on the package itself. When I asked the leader of the delegation to explain this, he told me, "We can count the number of scratches and see that the cartons are imperfect. No one knows what the juice is supposed to taste like!"

Walt with friends in Japan

Citrus World's international sales efforts were conducted on the same shoestring budget we had used when launching the Florida's Natural brand. Our competitors had divisions all around the world. We did all of our marketing and planning from Lake Wales. We had a separate international sales force, which never consisted of more than a manager and two regional salespeople, but it managed to succeed with our premium brand through innovation, creative negotiating, and a commitment to learning to manage in spite of cultural differences.

One of our first major markets for Florida's Natural was Mexico. We had been contacted by two Israeli expats, Haggai Blich and Yory Salant, who had established themselves in Mexico after arriving with nothing; in true entrepreneurial style, they had built their business over twenty-five years to become the largest importer of refrigerated high-end food products in that country.

At first, I thought the chances of success in Mexico were less than zero. Mexico has oranges that are of very good quality, and most people squeeze their own at home. But Yory and Haggai convinced Citrus World to try selling our juice in their country, and we quickly built our venture into a large business centered on high-end consumers who bought from Costco and Walmart. One of the positive effects of NAFTA was that it removed the duties on oranges imported into Mexico. But at the same time, it led to a major devaluation of the peso. In one period, the peso lost nearly 50 percent of its value in a short time.[2] This had the effect of raising the price of Florida's Natural by the same amount.

● ● ●

---

2 Jay Kaplan, "The 1994 Mexican Currency Crisis," *The 1994 Mexican Currency Crisis*, January 9, 1998, accessed July 7, 2016.
http://www.colorado.edu/economics/courses/econ2020/6550/readings/Mexico-currency.html

Haggai Blich observed that

> we had built a nice and growing business in Mexico, and then we were blindsided by the huge devaluation of the peso. Simply stated, we were unable to pay our invoices. We had bought the product at a higher-value peso and had to sell for lower-value pesos. One of the things I will always remember is my Lake Wales meeting with Walt. I knew that he was very direct and no-nonsense. I said to him, if you will give us extended terms, we will pay you every dollar we owe. And we will keep the business going once we can raise the prices in Mexico.
>
> Walt was either a gambler or a good judge of character. He looked me in the eye and said, "Okay, Haggai, don't screw me." This has led to 20 years of profitable business for both of us. And Walt is one of my favorite people. As I was getting ready to retire, Walt and I negotiated selling 50 percent of our distributorship to Florida's Natural. We agreed on a price of 4 million US dollars. Fortunately for me Steve Caruso turned the deal down. I say "fortunately" because nine months later, I sold my half to a European cheese company for seven million.[3]

WALT

In many markets, because of the short shelf life of Florida's Natural, it was impossible to distribute it before it passed the

---

3 Haggai Blich, interview by Walt Lincer, August 19, 2016.

expiration date. For that reason, our company had begun air freighting Florida's Natural to the United Arab Emirates. But the cost to transport each half gallon was about twelve dollars. We started negotiating with Nada Dairy in Saudi Arabia to produce the brand under license for the Gulf States.

The deal was finalized at the Food Marketing Institute Show in Chicago, and Mr. Alothman, the owner of the dairy, and his sons came to the show to sign the agreement. It led to a very interesting situation. On our side, there were the female sales manager and the female marketing manager, and on the other side was the Alothman family. But it quickly became obvious that our two females were not really paying attention to the paperwork. They were fixated on Mr. Alothman's ring. He had the largest diamond on his finger that I had ever seen.

I remember telling Mr. Alothman's son as he left the meeting to have his father put the ring in the safe because in Chicago, he might lose his hand.

I've visited the dairy in Saudi Arabia. It's the most amazing thing. Just think of the most desolate desert you've ever seen but with cows all over the place. But somehow, the Saudis make it work. I think at last count, the dairy had twenty thousand cows. The cows are shaded and sprayed with a mist of water to keep them cool in the summer, when the temperature sometimes reaches 125 degrees Fahrenheit. The milking is all done in air-conditioned barns.

Despite Tropicana trying several times to enter the Middle East market using the largest dairy, Florida's Natural's share continues to grow about 20 percent each year, and it has become one of our biggest export markets. We are the only not-from-concentrate premium juice sold in the high-end outlets.

In other countries, our company uses distributors who buy the product and then make sure it gets put on the shelves in the markets. In Singapore, we tried something new. We could not find a distributor who could handle our product successfully. So, we partnered with a local firm to start Florida's Natural Foods. The company started in what amounted to an oversized garage, with one truck. Citrus World and our local partner, the Lim family, contributed the original capital of $100,000. The company today not only distributes Florida's Natural but also distributes products for Danone, Nestle, and Pokka, and it now has sales in excess of $30 million and contributes profitably to our co-op's nonmember business. Citrus World now has dozens of dedicated trucks supplying every supermarket and convenience store in the island republic. We have added satellite distributors in Malaysia, China, and Indonesia. Recently, we have experienced significant growth in Central and South American markets. Although these markets had orange juice from concentrate, there were few or no premium not-from-concentrate options. New free trade agreements continue to open doors to expansion of the brand.

Many times, I have heard from Citrus World's grower-owners that they have discovered our products in off-the-beaten track locales like Tahiti or Hua Hin, Thailand. It is gratifying to think that our team is able to sell and ship products from Lake Wales, Florida, to all ends of the earth.

12

It Almost Seems Simple

When I retired from my executive position at Citrus World, I began reflecting on my experiences over the past thirty years. If you believe that everything happens for a reason, then it is easy to see how one step led to another for me. If you don't subscribe to that theory, then certainly the seeming randomness of the way my path unfolded might start to change your mind.

When I went back to college after the army, I had no idea of my direction. I happened into the *Readers' Digest* job and saw that I had a natural talent for sales. This, I learned, was called marketing. I saw that working hard, figuring out what products people wanted, and following my intuitions would be a good starting point. Then I learned by attaching myself to mentors who didn't always follow the straight and narrow path. When Dan Womack sold three sizes of fabric softener to customers in his territory, knowing that only two sizes existed, it told me that sometimes you have to be creative and find a way to step outside of the preordained boundaries. When

I joined Citrus World and saw the abysmal condition of its sales force, it taught me that you could learn from a negative example.

I found out a lot of things about myself too. For one, I don't like to be told what to do. And I don't like to be told what I can't do. When it seemed obvious to everyone that Citrus World couldn't possibly introduce a fresh-tasting not-from-concentrate juice in a market dominated by giants, it made me all the more determined to do it. When it seemed we would have to limit ourselves to working under the Donald Duck name, it made me more convinced than ever that we had to build a brand. And when we got knocked down repeatedly by the big juice companies that flexed their muscles and money and tried to shove us out, it made me certain that we could and should hang in there, that we would find a way to succeed.

Looking back over it all, it almost seems simple. Join a company that has been making juice for fifty years. Find the next consumer trend, which for us was not-from-concentrate juice. Then, put everything you have behind the effort. Obviously, these three sentences don't begin to cover the ups and downs and ins and outs of the company's day-to-day struggles, but on paper, it really was that simple.

SYL

Okay—maybe Walt thinks the whole process was simple, and I know he's not diminishing any of the hard work that went into creating and building the Florida's Natural brand. But I took away something else after looking over the stories in this chronology.

I noticed several places where the narrative describes Walt's ideas, some of which he attributed to things that had influenced him along the way. In fact, we can break down the key points in this book by grouping them into a few different Walt-centric touchstones.

"A MESSAGE TO GARCIA"
SYL

Walt talked about the impression the famous "Message to Garcia" essay made on him. The fact that a colonel could send one of his soldiers out to execute a difficult task without giving any hint as to how it could be accomplished showed Walt that this was the kind of person he wanted to be and the kind of person he wanted to have working for him. There are several examples of how this idea influenced his decisions and even enabled his brash behavior. When he asked Gap at HESCO to print packages in Barbados, Walt didn't care *how* he was going to do it. He didn't want to hear when there was a problem. He just expected it to be handled the way he wanted. And Gap, knowing that Walt wouldn't cut him any slack, figured out a way to make it happen. So what if it involved five pickup trucks heading to the airport at midnight? So what if the "international diplomacy" employed to convince the airline to remove its cargo and replace it with Fresh'N'Natural packages involved sums of money changing hands? So what if the project pushed the systems and employees to a near-breaking point? The job got done. No laws were broken, and no one got hurt. And not a single order for the nascent product was missed.

WALT

Okay—maybe I do lean heavily on people who work for me. But I also had a few bosses who did the same. Joe Marshburn and Steve Caruso challenged their employees to take responsibility for their jobs. Once they identified a goal, they cut us loose to achieve it. I wouldn't say the three of us shared the same management style, but this was a good example to follow. And there's another illustration of this way of thinking that Syl probably wouldn't mention. I learned early on that I could trust Syl. When I gave him the impossible task of preparing and delivering an ad to a remote sales meeting as his first assignment—and he made it happen—I knew that I had someone who would support me and execute the plans that I set forth. That was an invaluable part of the partnership. This is not to say that Syl just rolled over and saluted. We had plenty of disagreements and lots of discussions about how to achieve our goals. But once a plan was laid out, I knew he would carry it through without filling me in on all the details of how he was going to accomplish it. Because after all, that didn't matter to me. That's why I hired him. Believe me, I would have saved the money and handled it myself if I could have!

Lots of people think I am tough to work with. I admit I have a certain direct style. But I've learned one thing that may have come from my short time in the military. People want to know the mission. They want to be given concrete directions.

I don't think there was ever a time when my staff left a meeting unclear about our objectives. They may not have known how they were going to carry out the plan, but they certainly knew what it was. And carrying it out was their problem, not mine.

ATTITUDES DO NOT PREDICT BEHAVIOR
WALT

When I first got into marketing, I realized that there were two types of marketers: those who believed marketing was a measurable science, and those who regarded it as an art. I knew it was probably a mix of both, but I weighted it more heavily toward art. If marketing were that predictable, everyone would succeed. The best marketers rely on intuition. They trust their guts. Not everyone is cut out for marketing. If you don't have confidence in your instincts, then you are playing the wrong game.

Obviously, however, instincts can be wrong at times.

When Citrus World was still selling Donald Duck juice, we got an idea for a new licensed product. This one would be packed in juice boxes and aimed at kids and moms. It would compete with Hi-C and Juicy Juice. We thought we had a great plan for insuring its success: the product would contain 10 percent more pure fruit juice than Juicy Juice. Moms would love it. It would be healthier, with less added sugar and more nutrients. How could it lose?

We took it to focus groups and consumer trials and asked our target audience whether they would be willing to pay 10 cents more for a three-pack of juice. "Yes!" they told us.

"Absolutely!" they told us. They reinforced the importance of more pure juice, of feeding their kids more nutritional products. We walked away assuming that we had a winner on our hands.

Well, after only a few months, the product failed. In spite of our confidence in our research, and in spite of the positive way our groups responded to a juice that had more actual juice, adding ten cents to the price point sunk the product. This experience taught us the same lesson we should have learned with the Donald Duck juice block: attitudes do not predict behavior. I haven't forgotten this. Don't tell me what people say, tell me what they do.

THE ART OF WAR

SYL

Walt will be quick to tell you that I place too much stock in the influence *The Art of War* had on him. Well, maybe I should say instead that it influenced me. I read it on his suggestion, but I can honestly admit that I gained lots of insight into facing challenges and opportunities through the simple strategies laid out in this ancient book. It's an example of how powerful a message can be when it is boiled down to its most elemental points. When you read *The Art of War*, you find yourself saying, "Of course...of course." For the ideas are very straightforward, and even obvious in some cases. But the simplicity also showed me what Walt preaches: don't make it complicated.

The Art of War talks about strategies, tactics, positions, maneuvers, and attacks. And it especially covers finding opportunities through the weaknesses of the enemy. In each planning session the advertising and marketing teams started with an assessment of where our competitors were.

WALT

When the agency came up with our "Cold Facts" commercial, it was based on information we had uncovered about how Tropicana was using frozen juice in its mix, which positioned us to be closer to fresh. When we ran "Stripping Cartons," a commercial that claimed that taste tests had shown that our product was better, it played up our competitor's weakness—an outright attack on our part—but one that could be substantiated. And when we maneuvered our way into a new name and package without anyone—including our CEO, who was expecting it—recognizing that we had made a change, it showed that our strength lay in our flexibility, speed, and agility, which are not attributes commonly associated with lumbering giants.

A SMALL COMPANY CANNOT ACT LIKE A BIG COMPANY

SYL

Walt always reminded the team that a small company cannot act like a big company. We could not jump into the same pool as our large competitors; not in our advertising or strategy, not in our media plans, and on Citrus World's part, not in the products.

WALT

Citrus World was never going to be a big company. But we learned to use our size to our advantage.

At big corporations, people are forced to come up with innovations. I think part of the reason is job preservation. With so many people at each level, each marketing person has to show his or her creativity to stand out and move on to the next job. Hosts of employees feel the need to make contributions, so they introduce new products, create line extensions, or come up with new promotional schemes. These can be costly ideas. And in a large company, they are ideas that have to pass through many points for approval.

Having too many management layers often gets in the way of good relationships and speedy decision making. Early in my career, I made a decision about how I would structure a sales force if I ever had the chance to run one. I figured out early that sales and marketing teams needed to report to the same person. This would streamline operations and unite all players in a common cause. When I worked for Lever, I saw the disparity and the conflict between the goals of the sales department and the marketing group. I also saw how one group would work against the other to make itself look good. Everyone today talks about teamwork, and I know I have had that printed on more than one T-shirt for our sales meetings, but if you are not all working toward the same objective, your chance for success is greatly diminished. When Citrus World introduced Florida's Natural, *everyone* pulled together. We all had the same goal, and we all put that goal first. Those of us who were in on the launch won't forget how it felt to have our own brand and to see it spread from market to market, gaining share as it went. Because we were all directly involved, we all had ownership.

Whenever I could, I tried to use our company's size to our benefit, even though sometimes, we were pushed around a bit. When our competitors threw us into a broker crisis back in 2003, making us renegotiate with twenty long-time brokers, I realized that our size was not going to allow us to control the business the way the giants could. So, once the dust had settled and the critical issues were resolved, I determined that from then on, our sales department would only hire small brokers who would be involved in their individual markets and who would learn and respect our business. This was key—and it gave us much more control in the long run. When the broker situation presented itself, it was a disaster. But again, our flexibility and ability to shift directions helped us overall. Maneuverability again.

It was a funny thing that having all small regional brokers representing Florida's Natural gave us more leverage than having one national broker. If we had a weak broker in one market, we could change. Our competitors had no choice but to stay with one of the two national brokers.

VISION VERSUS STRATEGY
WALT

Citrus World could not have achieved the building of a national brand without the vision of its board. There were years when the board had to convince our growers to accept lower returns for their fruit while we put money back into Florida's Natural. The board had a vision of what the brand could be. But they relied on the company's executives and managers to have the strategy. When we reached national distribution, it showed that you need a steady application of both of these qualities.

With our limited budget, our team did not have the luxury of sitting around creating plan after plan for a never-ending series of new products that lasted a short time and lost money. I know that Minute Maid and Tropicana pictured themselves filling up the grocery shelves with line extensions, spin-off products, and new categories. All of those new products were designed to knock Florida's Natural off the shelves. The quick failure rate of many of those items only cleared the way for new ones the big companies were constantly introducing. I find it interesting that in looking back over those new product launches, very few remain in the market today. Each new product launch costs several million dollars. Our company never could have kept up with that as a way to keep the competition off the shelves. Each of our new products was designed to stay in the game for the long run. We held on by holding on—to our plans and our reality. Our large competitors envisioned wiping us out of the major grocery stores. We were backed by our board's vision, but we had a workable strategy for staying in.

SYL

Walt's focus on strategy helped the agency's creative and media-placement teams hit the target. Before my team and I would present to him, we had to drill down to see if the proposed work was hitting all the objectives. Walt put the team in its place once when we presented a document titled "Media Strategy." He took one look at it and said, "This isn't a strategy; it's a plan. There's a difference." We learned quickly how to tell the two apart.

FACTOR IN HUMAN NATURE
WALT

Some people think I am cheap. I'll be the first to admit that I am not extravagant and am always looking for a good deal. Maybe I learned a healthy respect for money at an early age. And I've already mentioned that I started my career by look-ing for a job that would enable me to make lots of money. So, when I started working for Citrus World, and I realized that it was a small company without a lot of cash to throw around, I knew it was a good fit for me. Even though I would be con-strained by budgets for most of my career, my ability to get the most I could out of each dollar spent helped me in the long run. I figured it was human nature to operate like this. And I was so sure that I was a good judge of human nature that when I went to that Winn Dixie manager long ago and offered him two free trailers full of Donald Duck chilled orange juice, I knew he would jump at the chance to take it. I couldn't imag-ine anyone turning down something that was free.

Sometimes human nature is unpredictable. But luckily, I was able to gauge it correctly some of the time. Take John Clarke, for example. When I first met John, I didn't quite know what to make of him. And when I sent him to the New York brokers, they *definitely* didn't know what to make of him. But one thing became obvious. Everyone liked John. He always had people around him laughing, smiling, and listening to what he said. And he had a way of getting people to do things for him. Lesson learned: it's human nature to like someone who makes people feel good. Let this person help you do your job. Let this person smooth the way after you deliver difficult news. It will pay off in the long run.

DON'T PAY PEANUTS

WALT

Armand Hammer of Occidental Petroleum once said, if you pay peanuts, you get monkeys. One of the keys to growing the FN brand was our incentive plan for the sales force. It allowed the sales manager who reached all of his or her objectives to earn a significant bonus. In the third year of the program, through no fault of the sales managers, no one earned a bonus. Our management team had misjudged the cost of fruit for the season and bought it at too high a price. We ended up being uncompetitive in our pricing that year to make up for it. Our sales force took the hit. I went to the VP of marketing and suggested that adjustments be made to the target so the sales managers could earn bonuses based on their efforts. I was told no in no uncertain terms. This turned out to be costly decision because one or two of our key managers walked out. After that, I made sure the sales force was paid if they performed.

IT'S SO OBVIOUS

WALT

I make decisions based on my intuitions. When I first went into marketing, I thought the field was BS and that I'd be a natural. Well, I guess I was a natural, but I don't think it's BS anymore. I think you have to have a gut feeling for what will work and what won't. I think you have to have a certain tolerance for risk and failure. And I think you have to trust yourself and the others around you to keep their fingers on the pulse of a situation so adjustments can be made. I guess these rules can be applied to almost all areas of life.

Common sense should also be seen as an extension—or even a confirmation—of intuition. It's probably a good thing that I was inexperienced when I began working with a big ad agency. I didn't know what to expect or what kinds of things were normal operating procedures. For example, when it was time to produce a new television spot, it was obvious to me that we wanted to be as cost effective as possible. That meant producing the spots locally, not having tons of people standing around doing nothing, and moving as quickly as possible through the production.

SYL

When Walt had our creative team use his own employees as the talent in Florida's Natural commercials, it was a perfect example of his gut instincts paying off. Since the ads were promoting the grower-owner message, and since we wanted people to see that we weren't some slick top-heavy company, it made perfect sense to use the co-op's own growers and even company sales people to represent us. There weren't any residuals or talent fees, and we got what we wanted. It was an obvious choice.

There was a time early in our collaboration when Walt's team and the agency's team were trying to figure out how to work together. The agency was trying to get to know Walt and his methods. Walt was trying to get to know the players in the agency's lineup and discover what we would bring to the table. And we were all struggling to figure out what to make of the new product. How should it be presented? What was its point of difference? What was the message? When we focused in on the grower-owner idea, it was another case of an obvious choice. In fact, it was so obvious that we nearly missed it. But it was right under our noses.

UNDERPROMISE AND OVERPERFORM

WALT

Every year, the sales, marketing and advertising teams worked on a plan that was developed from the bottom up. Each manager and the agency presented its ideas and goals for the upcoming season. The plan included all costs and expected results.

John Clarke and I would set the final objectives for the coming season. We made it a point to set reachable targets that would be easy to attain. We circulated the plan to the entire management staff and presented a condensed version to the board.

What no one knew was John and I never presented what we thought we could accomplish. We always sandbagged. If we said we would have a 5 percent increase but only reached 4 percent, we wouldn't have made the number. However, if we set the goal at 3 percent and reached 4 percent, we were heroes.

Year after year, we overachieved. Only one person, Frank Hunt, ever realized what we were doing. I distinctly remember him saying one day, "I know there's more. What's the real number for growth?" But he never held our feet to the fire. I guess he liked good news too.

HOW HARD COULD IT BE?

SYL

Walt is a piece of work. I can't count the number of meetings I've been in where he laid out an ambitious goal and walked out of the room asking the sometimes-stunned group, "How hard could it be?" The truth is, lots of things were plenty hard. Deadlines, budgets, creative approvals, media negotiations—none of these would define an easy day at the office. But to Walt, issues always boiled down to the simplest formula and his high expectations.

WALT

Look, this work is not rocket science. You create a brand; put brains, manpower, and money behind it; and then you try to move it forward in as straight a line as possible. Of course, there will always be bumps in the road, but overall, if you use your instincts and surround yourself with the right people, the path eventually straightens out.

SYL

Under Walt's direction, the Citrus World sales-and-marketing team built a solid partnership with our ad agency. And many friendships continue to this day. Good relationships also make a job easier. You don't want to disappoint a friend.

WALT

Building the Florida's Natural brand was one of the most interesting things I've done. I was in the right place at the right time when the opportunity came my way. And somehow, I surrounded myself with the right people, both inside my department and outside it, at the agency. Looking back at the overall scope of the group accomplishment, it's hard to believe we had the audacity to think we could go up against the giants in the juice industry and hold on to a number two or three position for years on end. But sometimes, it pays to just move ahead without overthinking or rethinking the process. Once we made the decision to go—we went. And I'm glad I was there as part of the team leading the charge.

Walt enjoying retirement

Epilogue

After retiring from Florida's Natural, Walt spent three years working as a consultant in Citrus World's international-trade division and no longer has any contact with the company. He now spends most of his time traveling, enjoying his grandchildren, and trying to keep all his digits while learning woodworking.

Syl is on a similar path, minus the woodworking. Since his retirement from 22squared, he has focused on maintaining his health and spending more time with friends and family.

In 2014, the new VP of marketing at Florida's Natural put the advertising account up for review. He fired 22squared via a FedExed letter in a curt culmination of a thirty-year relationship. Announcements about the hiring of the new agency failed to even acknowledge the longevity and productivity of the long association with 22squared and the fact that the agency had helped create and grow the flagship Florida's Natural brand. The subsequent advertising is taste-based and uses the tag line Great Taste Naturally. Early in 2016, Citrus World returned to the copy touting the All-Florida, Never Imported origin of the oranges. They also introduced several new products, none of which succeeded. Sales-volume decline has been in the double digits for the past few years.

Acknowledgments

At its heart, this book is about relationships.

So many people had a hand in creating the Florida's Natural brand that it would be impossible to name them all. But there are a few whose support and trust turned what at first seemed impossible to achieve into a long-running success story.

Many of these people were involved at the first glimmer of the idea to create a new brand of orange juice. Others, through their loyalty and faith in the process and the product, helped turn that glimmer into a steady glow.

As in the rest of the book, Syl and Walt each have a voice in the acknowledgments.

WALT

I suppose it's only fitting to start with the board of Citrus World. During my tenure, three of the four chairmen were able to steer our grower-members toward a shared vision for the company. Since Citrus World was a co-op, each board member was from a different, sometimes competing grower organization. Occasionally, the things we were suggesting, although they were designed to benefit the co-op as a whole, were not beneficial to one grower or another. I can't think of many incidents where that became a problem. When the different members walked in the door of the boardroom, they switched their grower hats for ones that said Citrus World. They all worked hard to reach agreement.

Once in a while, someone would say, "Well, that's not going to be good for my organization, but I can see why we have to do it." Early on, each person sacrificed his or her good returns to build the business.

Frank Hunt was chairman for nearly thirty years. We were lucky to have him. His father, Deely Hunt, was one of the founding members of the Florida Citrus Canner's Cooperative, which became Florida's Natural Growers. From the very beginning, Deely wanted to develop a brand that Citrus World owned. That dream was realized during the tenure of his son as chairman of the board. As a grower and as chairman, Frank shared this vision and put the Hunt Brothers, his organization, at the service of the co-op. Frank has a well-earned reputation for being highly ethical in his dealings and is a role model of what a chairman and a co-op member should be.

Dick (Richard) Fort Jr. came in during a period marked with major crises. Hurricanes, shrinking crop sizes, and a greening disease presented real challenges. He was a steady hand that kept the co-op moving forward. When the co-op struggled with fruit supply, he led the effort to gain new members. He also headed up the development of new mission statements to focus our member-growers and the company and reflect what the co-op was about. Finally, he refined the process for strategic planning, which aligned the company's and the growers' goals.

And Dennis Broadaway, Citrus World's current chairman, has always been a great supporter of the Florida's Natural brand. In spite of recent challenges with greening disease, new members are joining the cooperative because of the strength of the brand.

The board of Florida's Natural is a mixture of professional managers and grower families, some of whom have stayed on the board for generations. During my tenure, I saw many board positions pass from fathers to sons, and some of those fathers had inherited the jobs from their fathers. In the case of the Hunt family, Frank M. Hunt is the third generation to serve on the Citrus World board. Hill Griffin is another, following Ben Hill Griffin II and Ben Hill Griffin III.

Lindsay Raley succeeded his father, who was a quiet leader, building consensus on the board in tough times. Lindsay has stepped in to be a real leader of a new generation. Trying to name all the directors who helped build the brand is impossible, since that groundwork was being laid from the co-op's earliest years. Suffice it to say that with few exceptions, our board took risks and suffered initial low returns to make the brand succeed.

Senior Management

The many contributions of Joe Marshburn and Steve Caruso are detailed earlier in the book. The other senior manager who was very instrumental in growing the brand was Bob Behr. Dr. Bob, as we called him, was VP of technical services and planning and the COO. Bob was behind the scenes, ensuring we had sufficient fruit and production capacity to meet our sales needs.

Production Staff

The typical situation in almost any manufacturing company is that production is at odds with sales and marketing. Production management's goals are to produce at the lowest cost. Marketing's goals are to give customers what they want. Henry Ford was the typical product manager. He offered customers Model Ts in any color, as long as they only wanted black. Today, customers and consumers want products and services tailored to the needs of the day. Partly in response to the changing environment, Citrus World moved from being a production co-op to a marketing co-op.

At Florida's Natural, Charles Matthews and Carson Weeks, along with the whole production team, always rose to the challenges the marketing team threw at them, working to figure out how a job could be done rather than explaining why it couldn't. They sacrificed their goals to see that customers were satisfied.

The Fruit Supply Team

After Minute Maid became a division of Coca-Cola and Tropicana became a division of Pepsi, they no longer operated as stand-alone companies, which gave Citrus World a great advantage. When they were independent entities of those corporations, they had direct contact with the industry and with what was going on in the field. They lost a bit of that when they rolled into their parent corporations. One major problem for them, and an advantage for us, was that they couldn't always keep up with the sometimes rapidly changing fruit-supply situation.

After a major hurricane tore through Indian River, the grapefruit was literally blown off the trees. Dave Crumbly, Florida's Natural's vice president of agricultural services, immediately reported that fruit was on the ground and predicted a huge grapefruit shortage for the year.

That afternoon, Dave and his team started negotiating for grapefruit. Our sales managers immediately notified grocery buyers that there would be no promotions or deals for the season but that we would still be able to provide juice. Florida's Natural didn't miss one order.

Well, our competitors had no idea of the actual situation. They initially told the trade there was no shortage and that the business would go on as usual. Within a short time, they were allocating supply, shorting orders, and in some cases, stopping shipment of certain items altogether. This allowed Florida's Natural to become the number-one-selling brand of grapefruit juice.

The Sales Force

Shortly after I landed at Citrus World and took stock of the sales force, I knew I had work to do. I started by hiring Bob Sawatzki. Bob had hired and trained me at Lever Brothers, and he knew the refrigerated-foods business well. In fact, he knew every chilled-juice buyer better than the brokers did. I told Bob that we would have fun building a new brand. Since we were starting from nothing, I knew that for ten years, the process would be fun, since all the sales would be incremental. But after that—when our distribution began to grow significantly, then it turned into work. Bob was in on the first sales presentation on Florida's Natural and was instrumental in the rollout. He eventually became our national sales manager and was always a valuable part of the team.

Ken Stubbs is another sales professional I'd like to mention. He was quiet—really, he had the antithesis of a salesperson's personality. But he got the job done. Customers relied on him, and he delivered. Ultimately, he became the national accounts manager, responsible for all the major chains.

There are so many others on the sales team, but I'd like to mention those who were there at the beginning—or close to it:

- Rod Adamson
- Dale Mackey
- Barbara Nipper
- Susan Keane
- Marion Butler
- Bill Plyler
- Bonnie Hunter

The Food-Service Team

As the Florida's Natural brand developed, we worked hard to grow our away-from-home business, which was also known as food service. After Florida's Natural became a national brand, food service became more and more important to us. Now, it's the second biggest part of the business. Most of that is thanks to the efforts of these folks:

- David Jones
- Mike Smith
- Bill Watson
- Drew Eason

Brokers and Sales Agents

I have been lucky that my experiences at Citrus World have brought me into the larger world. In building its global business, I have traveled to many countries and made some long-lasting friendships, in particular with Rajan Warrior of Dubai. Rajan has shown his loyalty time and time again, often protecting me from making bad deals that may have harmed the company.

Citrus World's dealings with brokerage firms changed from time to time, but one broker in particular, Earl Keeter from Baltimore, moved from one brokerage to another to remain the Florida's Natural rep. He was totally loyal to our company and to the brand. Three customers Earl managed were very important to the start of the brand: Bernie Green, Carmen D'Ana, and Kenneth Herman. They supported us from the early days of Donald Duck to Florida's Natural.

Citrus World was always dependent on sales agents to know their individual markets. Like us, they built long-term relationships with customers, which contributed to our business. These folks helped us build our brand both nationally and globally.

- Larry Mastro
- Tom Boothby
- Hide Fujii
- Yoshi Fujii
- Robert Pritchard
- Danny Ramchandani
- Paul King
- Ailing Lim
- Lim Mah Tat

Other Florida's Natural employees who were invaluable to the team's efforts were

- Kay Gray and her staff in accounting;
- Gary De Witt and Jim Paulson and the IT staff;
- Kevin Gaffney and the research staff;
- Susan Langley and the HR staff;
- Dave Crumbley and the fruit procurement group;
- Tom Young and the staff in quality assurance; and
- Tom Abrado and the staff in traffic.

Outside Counsel

Over the years, I learned a lot from David Latham about trademark law and the various laws, like the Lanham Act and the Sherman Act, that protect consumers. And maybe he learned a little about marketing from me. Our running joke was that I liked making legal opinions, and he was always ready to expound on marketing strategies. Citrus World relied heavily on David, not only in the early days as we were finding our feet with Florida's Natural but also all along the long march to solid market share and national distribution. We often called on David to speak to the sales force at our national meetings. He delivered instruction and entertainment, with a great delivery of sometimes very dry material. He knew how to lighten up an evening party too. Once, the sales team had David referee a video horse race in a reward event for our best-vending brokers. They could make big money by betting on the outcome. During the main event, a tipsy David called the wrong winner. Unfortunately, there was no way to replay the race. David called it for the number-three horse, but the computer's calculations showed the number-four horse had won. He's famous for starting his scotch and soda at five o'clock. Unfortunately, this time, the scotch missed the winner.

ONE LAST WORD

Throughout the book, I have talked about the value, loyalty, and friendship that Syl brought to the Florida's Natural team. But there was one other way he helped us that I just have to mention.

The agency never exceeded its advertising budget when it was managed by Syl. It always left a reserve. This not only helped me build trust in him and his group, but it also let me earn the trust of my managers and the board. I was never questioned or held to the fire over the budget. They knew Syl and I would do and spend what we said we would.

SYL

Up and down the ranks, the agency's Florida's Natural's team was always incredible. Together, we shared the same attitude and goal; if we made the brand successful, the agency would be successful. Not only would we grow the account financially, but we would also add building a national brand to the agency's credentials. We didn't focus on winning awards for our advertising, although the times we did it was a nice bonus; we focused our efforts on building a unique brand image and moving the needle forward on all of Florida's Natural's measurements.

It is hard to find a starting point because as Walt said, there are so many people who had a hand in crafting the Florida's Natural brand. It would be impossible to name them all. But there are a few whose efforts so helped shape this brand into the incredible success story it is that they must be mentioned.

Chuck Mumah was our main creative guy for over eighteen years under four different executive creative directors. From crafting the original package design to seamlessly handling brand renaming to creating the iconic grower-to-consumer carton handoff, Chuck was a key player. Rest in peace, my friend.

Tobi Carvana and Catherine Durham created the initial grower-co-op campaign that served as the foundation for five sequential campaigns over the following ten years.

Kevin Botfeld was the creative leader in the All-Florida campaign. He also guided the transition back to the co-op message with the highly successful "Blossom" television spot.

Cheryl Howard, the team's long-standing print production manager, brought expertise in resourcing and budgeting and somehow managed to meet all those crazy deadlines!

Harry Vardis, director of research, provided leadership in navigating the team through the early years of taste tests and ongoing campaign development and brand-imagery studies.

Gerry Brewer put us at the front of the curve with the development of our customer database, including designing mechanisms to trigger brand loyalty.

Chris Tuff built on Gerry's foundation and guided us into the world of digital and social media. Florida's Natural was the first major orange-juice brand to reach over one million followers on Facebook.

Thanks to all those unsung media folks who made those consumer-reach and message-frequency estimates a reality. Special thanks to Gloria Peterson, Judy Popky, and Melanie Haley for their strategic guidance in effectively positioning our messages against competitors who spent up to three times our budget.

And thanks to account team members Jim Wyland, Ken Yarbrough, Brian Kirk, and Allie Clark for their contributions over the years.

On a personal note, without the leadership, support, vision, and mentoring from the following men, my role in this success story would not have happened:

- Knox Massey, former president and CEO of Tucker Wayne & Company and chairman of WestWayne Inc. (now known as 22squared Inc.): As I mentioned earlier, Knox plucked me from the print-production department and set me on a path to account management. Ultimately, he brought me on to help save the Citrus World account, a move that delivered me to the job that became the highlight of my thirty-eight-year career. And most importantly, he introduced me to Walt Lincer.

- Tom Fuller, CFO of 22squared: Tom mentored me on creating contracts, forecasting, and analyzing finances, and tolerated the many seemingly out-of-the-box requests made on behalf of the Florida's Natural account. Tom knew when to step in and when to step aside.

- Richard Ward, current president and CEO of 22squared: When Richard joined 22squared, he came with a vision of how to take the agency to the next level. Like Walt, he had the desire to take on the big boys. Because they shared similar business philosophies, Walt and Richard hit it off beautifully. Richard was always there if the account team needed him, but he let us continue doing what had worked so well. I'll always be indebted to Richard and Tom for their confidence in me to manage the account and the support they gave me at every turn, particularly as my health took a turn of its own.

And lastly, special thanks and gratitude to Sue Spann for her years of devotion to the team. From working full-time to part-time to being on-call twenty-four seven, Sue did it all. Her range included traditional account work, speech writing, video writing and production, and sales meetings scripting (including choreography of dancing sales managers), and she played a key role in cementing the client-agency relationship. She was a great partner and remains a great friend. Plus, without Sue, for Walt and me, this book would just be memories in our heads.

Susan Spann holds a degree in communications from Rutgers University. She has worked as a writer, an editor, an advertising account executive, a speechwriter, a writer/producer for film and television projects, and a translator.

In 1986, Susan began working with Syl Harris at an ad agency in Atlanta called Tucker Wayne and Company. There, she also connected with Walt Lincer and has worked with Walt and Syl ever since. Susan has been a part of the Florida's Natural brand since its inception, often charged with producing the results of Walt's and Syl's brainstorms.

Susan lives in Atlanta.